THE CELL CHURCH

LARRY STOCKSTILL

Regal

A Division of Gospel Light
Ventura, California, U.S.A.

Published by Regal Books
A Division of Gospel Light
Ventura, California, U.S.A.
Printed in U.S.A.

Regal Books is a ministry of Gospel Light, an evangelical Christian publisher dedicated to serving the local church. We believe God's vision for Gospel Light is to provide church leaders with biblical, user-friendly materials that will help them evangelize, disciple and minister to children, youth and families.

It is our prayer that this Regal book will help you discover biblical truth for your own life and help you meet the needs of others. May God richly bless you.

For a free catalog of resources from Regal Books/Gospel Light please contact your Christian supplier or call 1-800-4-GOSPEL.

Cover Design by Barbara LeVan Fisher
Interior Design by Britt Rocchio
Edited by Karen Kaufman

Library of Congress Cataloging-in-Publication Data
Stockstill, Larry 1953-
    The cell church/Larry Stockstill.
        p.   cm.
    Includes bibliographical references.
    ISBN 0-8307-2133-9 (ITPE).
    1. House churches. 1. Title.
    BV601.85.S76   1998   98-20950
    250—dc21   CIP

1 2 3 4 5 6 7 8 9 10 11 12 13 14 15 16 17 18 19 20 / 05 04 03 02 01 00 99 98

Rights for publishing this book in other languages are contracted by Gospel Literature International (GLINT). GLINT also provides technical help for the adaptation, translation and publishing of Bible study resources and books in scores of languages worldwide. For further information, contact GLINT, P.O. Box 4060, Ontario, CA 91761-1003, U.S.A., or the publisher.

This book is dedicated first to my father and mother,
Roy and Ruth Stockstill, whose 47 years of pastoral
ministry laid a firm foundation for ministry in my life.
I also dedicate it to my wife, Melanie, whose support and
patience in 22 years of mission work and pastoring have
been my inspiration; and to my six children whose lives
have been dramatically changed by cell ministry in the
last five years. Finally, I dedicate this book to the
24 Bethany pastors and wives, the 540 cell leaders
whose weekly sacrifice for souls is amazing,
and the 6,000 members of the church I
have attended since it began with only 12:
Bethany World Prayer Center.

CONTENTS

INTRODUCTION

If you had told me five years ago that I would be writing a book on "cell groups," I would have laughed in your face. I often recall the staff member who was "assigned" to oversee our 25 "Life Groups," asking, "Do you have any vision for our cell groups?" The truth is that I viewed these groups as one among our many ministries, a ministry "outlet" for frustrated leaders and a ministry "inlet" for frustrated megachurch members.

My "vision" for these monthly groups was that they continue to exist. "Ingrown," often "spontaneous," "fellowship based" and "routine" are words that described our groups. The leaders were precious and faithful, lacking only vision and direction. My only direction for cells came from "across the waters" in far away Oriental locations and polite nations where I thought the masses were accustomed to being herded and following their leaders.

In America, however, I understood too well the sense of independence, busyness and apathy toward anything other than Sunday morning Christianity. Besides, doing "another thing" with cells would have added to my already crowded schedule of preaching, counseling, staff direction, weekly media, school administration, missions oversight, building construction, ad infinitum. To "grow cells" would have been like adding a "growth"!

This book will surprise you. To know how far the Lord has

brought me in 60 months is awesome. I still have a heavy work-load, but it is offset by the joy of now having more than 540 ministry "teams" (cells). My focus and passion have been refined and directed into the twenty-first century with laser-beam precision. We were not expecting this exciting direction to occur in America, least of all in our church. However, we know it is the hand of the Lord getting our nation and all the nations of the world ready for the final harvest of souls.

Years ago, I loved to play with a little writing tablet that you could mark on with a plastic stylus. The sheet could be scribbled on until full, then with one jerk, the plastic sheet could be pulled up and erased. Perhaps right now your mental "sheet" is filled with tons of preconceptions and rationales about "cells." Before you read the first chapter, let God "lift your sheet" to a fresh page. Ask God to prepare your mind for a paradigm shift that could have you functioning as a "cell church" in 60 months.

Ezekiel saw a river whose depth could only be known by testing: "ankle deep, knee deep, loin deep, and waters to swim in." As you stand on the shore of church structure and ministry, pull off your "shoes" and stick in your big toe by reading this book. Look across the waters and you will see my head frolicking up and down, after five years, in the "waters to swim in." The waters are fine, safe, tested and biblical.

Come on in, I double-dog-dare you!

Larry Stockstill
March 1998

THE WIND
IS SHIFTING

It was the presidential election night, and thoughts of uncertainty crowded my mind. November 3, 1992 brought many Christians to a place of reckoning with the future and I was no exception. A new administration was being elected with uncharted moral and spiritual positions. As I prepared for bed, I felt strangely unsettled. It was as though I were standing on the edge of a precipice, uncertain about the kind of America we would know before the year 2000. I decided to just sit quietly before the Lord and meditate for a few minutes before retiring for the night.

THE VOICE I HAVE COME TO KNOW

As I slipped into my study shortly after midnight, a strange sense of destiny fell upon me. I had been unprepared for the way the Lord's presence would meet me there and totally alter the course of my ministry.

Although God has spoken to me often through an inner voice

rising from deep within my spirit which suddenly bursts into my conscious mind, I have never heard an "audible voice." I do, however, recall the first time I heard that inner voice in 1969 at the age of 16. I was emptying trash cans in my father's small auditorium, fulfilling my role as church janitor. As I stepped into the back doorway, a thought suddenly burst into my consciousness: *You know I have called you to preach, don't you?* It struck me with such force that I still remember the moment, including the wall color and every other minute detail of that experience. Within the week, I preached my first sermon.

Throughout the years, that voice has led me to Oral Roberts University, to marry my wife Melanie, to live in Africa as a missionary for two years and to return to Bethany as an associate pastor. When my father retired in 1983, I became the senior pastor of Bethany, and that voice directed me to construct our 6,000-seat auditorium while raising our missions budget $100,000 per year. By the end of 1992, the building and all 100 acres of Bethany became debt free and the congregation was giving 1.27 million dollars a year to missions.

Then, on that election night in 1992, the voice I have come to know and trust said, *Two things are coming in America: HARVEST and HOSTILITY. Your church is not prepared for either of them. I will show you something soon that will prepare you for what is coming upon the earth.* The force of the Lord's words was so overwhelming that I sat fixed in the chair of my study until almost 2 A.M. I realized God was changing something major in my life as the impression continued: *I am going to send a revival to America that will bring millions into the Kingdom. They will not walk, but run to Me.*

I recalled the sensation I had experienced during a crusade at Moscow Olympic Stadium in 1991, when I saw thousands *run* from the stadium bleachers to the altar. I remembered the tears streaming from my eyes as I watched people sprint unashamedly to the cross of Christ, thinking in that moment of how bankrupt and spiritually destitute we in America are. I had almost concluded after that crusade that my time was better spent overseas than in America, and that the United States was hopelessly doomed to be bypassed in the world revival. The election results that night had confirmed my concerns, so this word from the Lord was astounding to me indeed.

Another overriding thought pressed into my mind. The clear impression was, *A hostility will come against the Body of Christ in America causing believers to make adjustments in the traditional ways they have met together.* Clearly darkness and light are becoming so polarized in America that open hostility will eventually be released against believers in this nation.

> *With the cells in place,...even if the "trunk" of the tree were to be cut down, the "roots" of...cell groups would continue to flourish easily underground.*

I had read of the Church in China and how it had not only survived but also flourished in revival during periods of hostility. I had also read about the way Dr. Yonggi Cho, pastor of the world's largest church in Seoul, Korea, began his cell-church structure in the shadow of a North Korean invasion, realizing that an invasion would mean certain death to himself and his staff. Now, however, with the cells in place, Cho is assured that even if the "trunk" of the tree were to be cut down, the "roots" of his cell groups would continue to flourish easily underground.

PREPARING FOR HOSTILITY AND HARVEST

In the book of Genesis, God revealed to Joseph certain changes to make prior to the coming years of plenty and famine so he would have a plan of preparation to save Egypt. I don't like change, and frankly our church did not *need* a change in order to pull us "out of the ditch." We were seeing numerous people come to Christ each week and our financial house was well in order as a debt-free ministry. I realized that the word of the Lord to me was not a rebuke, but a *preparation* for change. I spent November contemplating the impressions of that election night, calling out to God to give me more insight.

My prayer was answered within the month while sitting in a restaurant with one of our former assistant pastors. As he began to question me about our present status as a church, I felt more and more uncomfortable with the "soft underbelly" issues he was uncovering. He grilled me on issues of how efficiently we were caring for our large congregation—then he made his "point." He began to testify about the transition his church was making to a "cell structure." In my mind I was comparing his description of cells to the floundering 25 cells we had "going" at Bethany. I really hoped he would change the subject, but he persisted. While sitting there, staring at my Mexican food, it suddenly dawned upon me that his probing words were not his own but were from the Holy Spirit.

The one-way "conversation" ended about an hour later with his recommendation to read Dr. Ralph Neighbour's book *Where Do We Go from Here?* (Touch Publications). I spent the end of November and the first of December reading the book, nearly infuriated by its message. I was frankly outraged at how easily Neighbour disposed of the traditional American church and described a new paradigm of church structure called the "cell church."

Gradually, my anger turned to intrigue as the book explained how the principles of the Early Church in Acts have birthed huge cell churches throughout the world today. The birth of these churches has been accomplished by plugging people into life-producing home groups consisting of 6 to 12 people. Each group then comes together once or twice a week with all the other "cells" into a "celebration," something similar to the congregational meetings I was accustomed to. It was the simple approach of the Early Church in the "temple" and "house to house." My doubting disposition gave way to a soft reverence for something awesome and supernatural.

Chapter by chapter, Dr. Neighbour, one of the pioneers of the Cell Church Movement and founder of Touch Outreach Ministries, described the cell churches around the world. My avid interest in missions coupled with a background as a former missionary to West Africa had given me a deep respect for our brethren in other nations. Snatches of testimony from what Dr. Yonggi Cho had achieved in Korea through cells had obviously reached my ears, but I had dismissed them offhand as peculiar to the Korean culture.

Dr. Neighbour, however, had so many similar stories that I was forced to rethink the concept of cells. From the Ivory Coast, to Manila, to El Salvador and of course, Korea, the story was the same: the major "megachurches" of the world have changed their structures to accommodate massive harvest. Dr. Neighbour's theme was simple: the traditional, program-based church-ministry structure cannot contain the coming revival.

Bethany's structure was already pretty simple. Our motto had always been "Simplicity, Sincerity and Sacrifice." Our government consisted of three outside pastoral presbyters, three staff elders and three congregational deacons to allow for flexibility and accountability. These nine members of our board of directors were wide open for any biblical, ethical and practical direction from the Lord.

I finally developed a deep inner witness that moved me forward with total confidence. Thus, somewhere in the soul-searching of the first two weeks of December, 1992, I became fully persuaded that cells would work in America, and especially at Bethany. I had no American pattern or model to visit and emulate, but I did have a great staff of sacrificial pastors, a joyful church with a missions vision and a handbook written by a man with more than 25 years of experience in cells.

A NEW PARADIGM

Bethany's annual planning retreat that December was interesting, to say the least. I spent an entire day presenting the "cell church" paradigm to our pastors, describing their future new roles, and casting vision and faith before them. At first, my staff all looked at me as though I had come from another planet! Finally, they caught the vision and we planned 12 weeks of training which would begin in January, 1993.

When the new year rolled around, I called together the group of 500 intercessors we had trained throughout the years and dubbed the "Gideon's Army." For years the "Gideon's Army" had been meeting every Saturday morning from 9:00 to 10:00 A.M. to pray for the pastors, church services, ministries, missionaries and the breaking of spiritual strongholds in Baton Rouge. I knew this group was to be the "core"—anyone who would come on a Saturday morning to pray had to be open to the new direction the Holy Spirit was showing us! I called together all 500 intercessors (including our existing 25 home group leaders) and started training them from the second chapter of Acts.

A NEW YEAR, A NEW SEASON

I will never forget that first week of January, 1993! It was as though the seasons had changed at Bethany. In that week we paid off the balance of our church mortgage 10 years early and became debt free. The church was ecstatic about our new financial freedom and excited about new opportunities. The members fully trusted my leadership as I announced to those 500 faithful intercessors that we were going to become a cell-based church with cells meeting weekly instead of monthly.

Our focus would be on moving new converts and visitors, the growing edge of the church, into cells in order to provide them with a sense of family and a safe place to be personally discipled. We recognized that many of our existing members already had their established relationships and did not feel a need for a cell, as did new believers or visitors. We stressed that people would not be treated as "second-class Christians" if they did not want to attend a cell. The excitement grew as week after week we imparted the vision of weekly cells.

As I previously mentioned, Bethany already had home groups, much the same as many other American congregations do. The "home group ministry" was there to accommodate the cry of a few who needed "more fellowship." Other members were more oriented to a congregational meeting. Thus, our 25 cell groups had been meeting monthly (most out of wanting to please me), and a group occasionally multiplied by accident!

The "home group ministry" as we had known it was about to change. The leaders began to envision an entirely different kind of cell: an evangelistic, multiplying, life-giving cell. During those 12 weeks of training, two new streams of cell "revelation" ignited my "spark" of vision into an inferno. The first stream of revelation began to flow on a trip to Singapore and Korea.

THE SINGAPORE PROTOTYPE

In March 1993, I attended a cell conference in Singapore hosted by Dr. Ralph Neighbour and Lawrence Khong, pastor of the dynamic Faith Community Baptist Church. The conference had a dramatic effect upon me. I observed a "cell church" with 400 cell groups and 6,000 members. There were no church programs—only cells. During a sleepy, low-key afternoon session (that I almost skipped) I saw one of the "District Offices." These offices were geographical nerve centers where one "District" and numerous "Zone" pastors supervised one geographical area of Singapore. The goals, vision and "cell leader" growth graphs were posted on the wall in full view of everyone. The office staff spoke of "conquest," like a military strategy room in the Pentagon.

The District pastor's desk was in a separate office and the Zone pastors were in a large open room with their cell strategy mounted on the wall for all to see. I had heard of cells, but this was militant! Here was a highly motivated, focused church with a vision to plant a cell on every block in Singapore by the year 2000! The happy, efficient staff was moving in powerful unity, and the effect on the 800 delegates from America and other nations was riveting.

I completed my trip with a stop at Dr. Yonggi Cho's church in Seoul, Korea, and observed his "District Offices" at work in that 750,000-member church. People stood in line by each Zone pastor's desk after service for prayer and counseling. I wondered, *Why have I never seen a "District Office" in America? Could this serve as a spiritual "Command Post" where the invisible cell structure could become visible and cell leaders could find their "address" in the church?*

I purposed to remodel when I returned to Bethany. Four little-used rooms in our back nursery hallway became our first "District Offices" for cells. Plans began immediately for a permanent "Touch Center" where the cells could be nurtured and constantly motivated.

EVANGELISTIC CELLS, A CURE FOR *"KOINONITIS"*

The second stream of revelation that merged in my mind was that of "evangelistic cells." My traveling companions to the Orient in March had been two Mexican blood brothers and pastors, Victor and Noe Martinez. These two deeply spiritual leaders supervise megachurches in Monterrey and Mexico City. On the long plane rides, the Martinez brothers spoke to me in detail about the idea of "evangelistic cells." They had spent three weeks studying a remarkable cell church with more than 50,000 members and 4,500 cell groups in San Salvador, El Salvador.

The growth of the San Salvadorean cells comes from *two* weekly cell meetings: one on Tuesday and one on Saturday. The cell-meeting format alternates based upon the purpose of the meeting. The first meeting on Tuesday night is for "edification" (to edify the cell members and to plan an evangelism meeting for the following Saturday). The second meeting on Saturday night is the actual "evangelism" meeting (inviting the lost, not just believers). The alternating effect of these two different formats creates a dynamic like a piston or a rifle! The group can "recoil" (rest, minister to each other and plan) on Tuesday (as the hammer is pulled back), then "shoot" (evangelize their lost friends and neighbors) on Saturday. This alternating dynamic keeps the groups focused and powerful.

Purpose and focus prevent the cell group from degenerating into a "care group" mentality where the goal is simply fellowship and refreshments. The two essential elements of cells, edification and evangelism, are beautifully integrated. With such a life-giving foundation, I could see that it would be impossible for this kind of group to come down with the cell group disease American pastors laughingly refer to as "*koinonitis*" (ingrown fellowship disease).

I combined the idea of a geographical "District Office" from Singapore with the evangelistic focus of El Salvador, alternating "edification and evangelism" in two distinct formats. We chose to have each format alternate every other week instead of within a week. By the end of the 12 weeks, not only had the leaders caught vision and established clear direction, but the four nursery rooms were also fully remodeled to serve as "District Offices." Easter 1993 was a great day at Bethany. We called forward the 54 new cell leaders and announced our intentions to transition our church to a cell church within a five-year time frame.

We assured the congregation that the groups would focus on new converts and visitors but that everyone was welcome to attend the new "Touch Groups" (or "Cell Groups"). The church rejoiced in forming a nurturing way to care for new believers, and the new leaders were released into ministry. Their mission was to multiply within six months by birthing a new group of 6 to 12 members. Every new contact made for Bethany from any source was to be channeled into their hands for follow-up. So much has happened since that Easter that many of the details have blurred.

"Coincidentally," Dr. Cho had a sudden opening in his speaking schedule in the United States a week later. He ministered at Bethany on a Sunday evening and more than 4,000 believers listened as he spoke about prayer and its power in the cell church.

Dr. Cho's message was, needless to say, a home run! We seemed to enter into a spiritual "zone" that has continued unabated for the past five years.

CLOSING THE BACK
DOOR TO THE CHURCH

Within six months, the 54 cell groups had multiplied into 108 groups. Their growth came primarily from assimilating Bethany members who developed an interest in the revival fire and soul-winning passion the groups exhibited. Another interesting phenomenon emerged. A study of giving records showed that from the years 1990 to 1992, Bethany had not actually grown. (Fifty new families did join each month through the "front door," but obviously an equal number left out the "back door.")

That same study showed that by year-end 1993, our first year of cell ministry, a net growth of 600 new families were added to the church! The cell groups had helped to close Bethany's "back door." The years 1994 through 1996 showed a similar increase of 400 to 600 additional new families each year, and a growth of 200 additional cells. We ended 1996 with 310 cell groups and 2,000 more families than when we began in 1993.

At Bethany, the case for the "cell church" is closed. The Bethany people are being pastored better than ever. They all have a format to evangelize their friends; they are also finding places for their leadership skills.

GET READY OR GET RUN OVER!

These five years have been years of learning. We have made mistakes, but gained experience each time. The process of cell *evangelism, assimilation, discipling* and *planting* has been worked and reworked to make our leadership training adequate to prepare the church spiritually and numerically for the harvest. In each of our "cell church" conferences, we have informed the delegates in the opening session that "we really don't know what we are doing!"

Much of our success has been the product of "trial and error."
For example, 10 months after Bethany began cells, our *leading*
from the Lord about preparing for a coming massive harvest in
America became a tangible *mandate*. We hosted the Canadian-
based drama, "Heaven's Gates and Hell's Flames." What began as
a three-night Christian drama about heaven and hell resulted in
900 conversions the first night! The drama extended week after
week, and people arrived up to four hours early to attend the
capacity crowds of 6,000 nightly. As many as 1,200 *ran* forward
each night to repent and turn to the Lord.

Within that 21-night period, we registered 18,290 decisions for
Christ! The 120 newly formed cells worked tirelessly to contact
the new believers. Our office staff worked long hours recording
names and addresses, generating follow-up cards, organizing
phone banks and beginning new convert classes. The traditional
program "net" of the church stretched, strained and broke under
the catch of "fish." Believe it or not, we got tired of harvesting!
Everything was overwhelmed.

We sent each decision card to the local Baton Rouge church
where an indication appeared on the card that a person had ever
attended that church. Thousands of cards were mailed. Though we
retained at least 5 percent of that massive harvest, much of it was
lost forever and the message was clear: *Get ready or get run over.*

Through all of our mistakes and growth, we have held to one
central tenet: *The Church must get ready for revival.* The work of
pastoral care, evangelism and leadership training must be done
through some structure, and we find the cell-church structure to
be the simplest and most expandable method of performing
those functions.

At the time of this writing, a revival at Brownsville Assembly
of God in Pensacola, Florida, has continued unabated for 27
months. More than 100,000 decisions have been recorded, and a
church with a seating capacity of 2,600 has often had 7,000 in
nightly attendance in overflow chapels and even outdoor tents.
Thousands line up all day and even sleep all night on the church
parking lot just to get a seat. Similar moves of God are breaking

out nationwide and worldwide as the showers of revival ripen the final harvest. I firmly believe that by the year 2000 America will be in the flames of mighty repentance and revival.

We sometimes see 50 conversions at Bethany on Sunday morning and 25 on Wednesday evening. *We must prepare if we are going to be ready for the coming harvest.* The traditional structure of evangelizing, assimilating, discipling and releasing leaders will never be fast enough or efficient enough to keep pace. As it was with Moses, so it will be with us...

A LESSON FROM THE WILDERNESS

Not long after Moses led the Israelites out of Egypt, it became apparent that the structure for managing such a multitude had to change. Needing simple counsel and direction, the people waited in long lines at Moses' tent. This wore the people out and exhausted Moses. Moses' father-in-law instilled in him the timeless principle of delegation and oversight. He arranged the "church in the wilderness" into teams of 10s, 50s, 100s and 1000s. Only the hard cases reached Moses' attention. This pastoral system proved to be enormously efficient as 3 million people marched, moved and warred together with no public address system or electronic mail!

Moving people into relationship and oversight is the time-proven method of pastoring people. Why had I previously failed to see that the Early Church accommodated harvest immediately by meeting "house to house" (see Acts 2:46)? Is our culture exempt from the biblical principles that held the Early Church together and now works beautifully in many other cultures throughout the world?

As you read this book, open your heart and mind to a whole new world of church structure: a structure so simple that the Early Church could do it with no computers, zip codes or facilities. The "cell church" is already harvesting and holding multitudes in churches worldwide, and the question is: Can it work in America? I believe it can, and the next few chapters will describe how one American congregation has been radically transformed. Get ready for the journey: *harvest* and *hostility* are coming. Will you be ready?

CHURCHES WITH WINDOWS

The richest man in the world is Bill Gates, owner of the powerful Microsoft corporation. This young man's personal worth is more than $39 billion. Gates earned his vast fortune with a small idea that revolutionized the world of home computers: *Windows*. Previously, computer users only had a "menu" of programs from which to make their selections. Each program worked independently of the others and had to be separately opened and closed before another program could be accessed. This awkward arrangement existed because the various programs did not speak the same "language." The programs were physically inside the same computer but totally incompatible.

The computer reformation began when Gates discovered a way to make all programs speak the same "language" and remain "open" simultaneously by occupying small "windows" on the computer screen like the windowpanes in large living room windows. Each program's "windowpane" is represented on the screen by a small logo or "icon." By pointing an arrow and clicking a computer mouse, each or all of the programs can be opened and remain open so the operator can move rapidly between them. The programs are unique, but able to "talk" to each other because they are in the same "environment."

Thanks to Gates's genius, working with a home computer is now fun, fast and focused. You don't have to shut down your Bible program to work on your word-processing program for a Sunday sermon. A host of programs can be "loaded up" simultaneously and used in tandem for maximum efficiency. Could "cells" be a similar "operating system" to simplify church structure and make it fun again?

SIMPLIFYING CHURCH STRUCTURE

Few problems frustrate a pastor more than having a number of competing programs within the church. The focus of the staff members is skewed in pursuit of their particular programs. Program leaders all vie for the senior pastor's attention and budgetary priorities. Because the volunteer base rarely changes, the leaders all try to woo the same volunteers into their programs. Staff meetings become emotionally charged over what is *truly* important. The pastor is bewildered in deciding which program to give creative energy to while trying to juggle important pulpit and family responsibilities. New members are moved down the process line from program to program, often falling through the cracks before being truly assimilated into church life. The landscape of the church's programs is replete with so many different methods and philosophies that it can almost cause you to think you are a member of many different churches.

Can you imagine what would happen if all the church programs were changed to a common format or "environment"? What if all staff members were performing their ministry functions in the same way while targeting different groups within the church? The pastor could then focus on the "environment" of ministry and motivate the program leaders to growth within that common format. All staff would be singularly focused on common principles, and budget would be allocated based upon the size and responsibilities of each area. Nothing would compete for volunteers and spotlight. Pastoral staff would know exactly who they were pastoring and how their performance would be evaluated. The ease of pastoring such a structure would quickly be obvious to anyone who has ever tried to fit the multitude of American church programs into any kind of manageable structure.

Is it any wonder that Dr. Yonggi Cho's church has been able to grow to 750,000 members with 25,000 cell groups, and that Dr. Cho says he has to look around the office to find something to

> *I have learned that true genius is not the ability to make things complex, but the ability to make them simple.*

do? Is it possible that Pastor Dion Robert of Côte d'Ivoire (formerly the Ivory Coast), West Africa, can pastor 120,000 members in 8,000 cell groups with no computers or zip codes?

The cell church is not just about getting people to have refreshments together in homes but a simplification of church structure that powerfully focuses everyone on the same thing. I have learned that true genius is not the ability to make things complex, but the ability to make them simple. Any child can take *all* the toys out of the toy closet and clutter the room. Only an adult can keep the room simple and uncluttered. We live in a nation where "crosstown competition" often spawns programs the Lord did not birth and we cannot maintain. Tired pastors start and stop the newest facility and volunteer-based "programs." They run from conference to conference, implementing each new program while stretching their tired staffs across four or five unrelated areas of ministry. We must simplify.

FILLING IN THE CRACKS WITH "SHARED RESPONSIBILITY"

This simplification of structure is illustrated in the transition of Bethany's "follow-up" system from program based to cell based. The program's process previously began when a person responded to the invitation for personal ministry at the end of a service. The new believer was sent into a room for ministry and asked to fill out an information card. That information was then given to the "follow-up program" where contact was made by a church leader within the next few days. Next, the card was passed on to a pastor who led a Spiritual Foundations class, which the person, hopefully, attended. The Spiritual Foundations program sent the card to a home group. A few other steps were thrown into the process as well, but the bottom line was that hundreds of converts were going in and yet few disciples were coming out.

Our process looked fine on paper, but it was awkward, to say the least. The volunteers who managed each stage of the process had no relational "connection" with the new converts. Their attention focused each week on the "newest converts" from the previous Sunday. As a result, those new believers who were already in the process often fell through the cracks.

As you can imagine, it was difficult to hold the harvest. Federal and state programs often operate in much the same way with unrelated agencies trying to meet needs with overlapping and even conflicting criterion. This faulty system has proven to be a disaster in government, and almost as bad in our churches.

With a cell structure, however, the situation is drastically improved. When an individual comes to the Lord in a service, a cell leader stands behind that person at the forefront of the altar. After prayer, the new believer is led upstairs to our District Offices and greeted by a person acting much like an airline agent greeting an arriving flight. The person is asked for his or her zip code, then directed with the cell leader/counselor into one of seven District Offices based upon that person's address. The new believer views a short video on Bethany and cell life and is then introduced to the appropriate Zone pastor. The person gets "Jesus" and "cells" at the same time! New believers have no built-in bias against cells, but are thrilled to have a support group and spiritual family to help them in their new walk.

Within 24 hours a pastor and a cell leader visit the new believer's home to invite that person to the nearest group. Of course, if the individual has been brought to church with a cell member, he or she is assigned to that cell member's group. Relationship is formed, the follow-up process starts and bonding with real Christians begins. No longer are people part of the "program"; instead, they are in a natural, loving environment where they can be discipled and actually released into leadership themselves.

Using this method, Bethany has gradually replaced all its programs with cells within the past four years. We still have all the functions of our former programs; however, all that the former programs did is now accomplished through cells. Through the use of what we term "shared responsibility" all functions of church work are spread across the entire cell structure. Each cell knows its function in pastoral care, following up new believers, helping at services, praying for missionaries, helping in outreaches and all the working functions of the local church. Each cell does a spiritual gifts analysis to help members find their place in church life. Their gifts are released in the cell environment weekly and in the congregational environment quarterly (more on this in chapter 3).

THE CELL CHURCH VERSUS A CHURCH WITH CELLS

You can readily see that we are not talking about a "church with cells," but a "cell church." The cells are not an appendage, demanding attention like all the other programs: they ARE the program. As the pastor of a church with cells, I was like the juggler who performed on the Ed Sullivan show years ago. He could spin a plate and put it on a stick, repeating that process 15 to 20

times. The catch was, however, that the juggler had to constantly run back and forth to spin each plate or it would fall. His personal momentum was necessary to keep all the plates aloft.

What a picture of the typical pastor! All programs require the
pastor's personal "momentum" and attention or soon the volunteers lose interest. Staff members beg the pastor to come to their
volunteer banquets, mention their ministries from the pulpit and
infuse their programs with fresh ideas. The pastor's already over-
loaded brain is always "spinning plates," worrying about which
one is wobbling and about to come crashing down! I can truth-
fully say that the exasperation of "multiple plate spinning" has
ended for me. I am now focusing my energy, vision and attention
on the one plate that is carrying the purposes of the church: our
cell groups.

Bethany today is like the screen of a *Microsoft Windows*
computer environment. All of the former programs at Bethany
are still visible, but they have all been changed to a common format. Benevolence, follow-up, hospital visitation, outreach,
youth, singles, intercession, fellowship meals, workdays, usher-
ing/greeting/parking lot, and a host of other church functions are
accomplished each week by cells. The awkward, competing environment is gone and a simple "Early Church feeling" is present.
The cell process may seem like an oversimplification, but it is
working beautifully at Bethany. The most beautiful part is that
the same structure will meet our needs, even if we grow phe-
nomenally into the next century.

NEW PERSPECTIVES FOR "DOING" CHURCH

The "cell church" may require a "paradigm shift." A "paradigm"
controls how we interpret what we see and experience. It con-
sists of a whole set of perspectives. The following drawing illustrates how a shift of perspectives works. Look carefully at this
illustration. It can be seen as an old lady with a large protruding
chin looking down, or as a beautiful young lady looking away

from you over her right shoulder. Depending on which you see first, it is quite difficult to then see the illustration the other way. Many perspective shifts, which usually require effort and a stretch to perceive things differently, lead to a "paradigm shift."

We perceive an entire branch or branches of reality differently.

We have often seen the church as a set of programs rather than a set of relationships. The "home groups" were "care groups" or some branch of ministry in the church. The paradigm shift we must make is to begin to see the cells as "the church." In Bogota, Colombia, the International Charismatic Mission is evangelizing that major city of 6 million people through cell groups. Its church growth yielded 1,500 cells in 1994; 4,500 cells in 1995; and as of this writing in 1998, has 14,000 cells! The ICM's youth group has 6,600 cells, and the youth alone are winning 600 new converts per week! I know we have some pretty dandy programs in America, but what is producing fruit like that?

PRUNING CHURCH "SUCKERS"

Tomato plants have small branches that grow in the "forks" off the main stalk. These small, unproductive branches are called "suckers," because they are not actually fruit bearing but simply pulling life from the main branches. If they are not pruned, only very small tomatoes will grow on the ends of the real branches. How many "suckers" are there in our ministries which are sapping finances, energy and time without fulfilling the Great Commission? In chapter 9 we will deal with how to transition each program to cells, but the issue here is: Can we transition these programs and still fulfill the same ministry functions?

The answer is yes. The transition will take time and require careful pastoral skills. You must be patient and see the long-range goal. I can testify, however, that to sit in a staff meeting now with 24 pastors who have *nothing* to discuss but cells is wonderful beyond description. Our pastors are happy, our members are happy, our newcomers are happy, *my wife is happy*, the city is being impacted weekly in more than 540 cell-group locations and who knows what God has for us in the future.

CELLS: THE NEW WORLD STANDARD

Not only has our own ministry been revolutionized, but the cell structure is also being duplicated in the worldwide mission works with which we are connected. In Nairobi, Kenya, Pastor Donald Matheny's church of 1,200 members was meeting in the Intercontinental Hotel. The 10-year-old church had grown into three services but could not retain the vast numbers of people coming to the Lord. In August of 1994, Pastor Matheny returned from our National Cell Church conference and implemented the cell structure. Within three years, his church has moved to an outdoor stadium with 3,500 attending each Sunday. The Nairobi Lighthouse Church now has more than 2,500 attending its 450 cells and an average of 350 people per month are being led to the Lord *in cells.*

The cell structure is a system of church operation that is rapidly becoming a world standard. This new "cell system" could be compared to the takeover of the American "standard system" of measurement by the international "metric system." Our staff can quickly and easily coordinate and glean from the staff members of cell churches in South Africa, the Philippines, Thailand, El Salvador, Singapore, Colombia, Korea, Mexico or any of the other nations where the cell structure is in place.

With some exceptions, the present church structures of America are seen as unwieldy and impossible to implement in other less "sophisticated" cultures around the world. A decentralized, lay-driven ministry structure has served the Chinese church throughout 50 years of persecution and was behind the astonishing growth of the Ethiopian church during 10 years of Communist persecution. The bright, innovative leaders of the world-class cell churches hardly look up now to notice an American church of 10 to 15,000; they are pastoring between 50,000 and 100,000 believers and more. God has blessed Bethany's present structure, but are we open to a multiplication of that number?

A paradigm shift will definitely be required in order to rethink our precious traditions of pastoring, evangelizing and training: the revival at hand leaves us no other choice! Jesus told Peter to let down the "nets" (plural) and his response was with a "net" (see Luke 5:4,5, KJV). The result was predictable: their net broke. Could it be that God is giving us fresh insight and revelation into a larger net, a net that can catch and hold the "great multitude of fishes." As we look at the major functions of the local church (pastoring, evangelizing and training leaders), compare your present structure and honestly evaluate how effective it is in these three functions.

Using our present slow and complicated church structures, a mighty rush of revival in America would leave us unprepared to hold and disciple the harvest. I read once about a CEO of a Fortune 500 company who threw out 22½ inches of policy manuals in favor of a one-page philosophy statement.[1] All of the cumbersome, complicated procedures were summed up in a simple new philosophy of doing business. It obviously takes management skills to manage cells, but the job is easier when everyone is focused on performing the same task with the same philosophy.

Let's get ready to change. Let's hitch the wagons, join hands, bow our heads and ask God to help us make this cell system work in America. America is coming into revival. Within the next five years, millions will be joining the Body of Christ, and they will need to be discipled and sent out. Open your heart and get out your notepad...maybe Bill Gates has something after all.

Note

1. Thomas J. Peters and Robert H. Waterman, Jr., *In Search of Excellence: Lessons from America's Best-Run Companies* (New York: Warner Books, 1984), p. 65.

PARTNERSHIP

"Partnership" was a concept Jesus understood. He and His disciples walked the length and breadth of Israel as a tightly knit team. Through dangers, difficulties and rejection, the Twelve refused to separate when others became squeamish about following Christ. Many of the disciples were already in partnership when Jesus called them. The story of the filled and breaking fishing net in Luke 5 illustrates that Andrew, James and John were "partners with Simon [Peter]" (v. 10, *KJV*). These men had learned that their productivity increased dramatically when they used a *net* corporately rather than a *hook* individually.

A recent trend in corporate management is the concept of "team management." Team management involves tackling problems as groups rather than relying upon individuals for solutions. The corporate world is benefiting from a biblical concept: "Two are better than one, because they have a good return for their work" (Eccles. 4:9).

I now believe that the team concept is at the bedrock of the answer to "Why cells?" Ask yourself: Can we pastor our churches more effectively when people are disconnected individuals or when they are in ministry "teams"? Are believers as spiritually productive alone as they are in groups? Do people backslide, divorce and fall away from the Lord as often in accountability groups as they do when they are on their own? Surely every sincere pastor has wrestled with these questions, therefore, this chapter is devoted to explaining the "Principles of Partnership."

JESUS' FIVE PRINCIPLES OF PARTNERSHIP

John 13—17 records the final teachings of Christ before His death. Closeted together in an upper room, the Twelve listened as the Master trained them for the future. With seeds of division and individualism already present among His disciples, Jesus used this last teaching to lay out in nugget form the principles of partnership that would keep them together in His absence. Concept by concept, Jesus dissolved their personal agendas and prepared the men to act as a unit. This is, in essence, what a cell is: a group of people who have laid down their personal agendas to work together as a team.

1. Serving
Jesus' first principle, in John 13, involved "serving." The disciples had all passed by the menial wash basin at the door, judging themselves too important to wash each others' feet. While they conjectured about their positions in the new Kingdom, Christ quietly slipped away and later appeared at their feet with His coat removed and a towel in His hand.

Peter was indignant and refused the Lord's service. Christ replied, "Unless I wash you, you have no *part* with me" (v. 8, italics added). The word "part" in this verse comes from the Greek word *meros*, which means "a division or share." Jesus was essentially saying, "If I don't serve you, we are not partners." All partnership is based primarily upon a willingness to surrender personal promotion rights and to look seriously at the needs of another.

Preaching on the virtue of serving others is important, but how many people put into practice what they've heard? Their question is, "Where and whom do I serve?" After a powerful sermon on the good Samaritan, how many of our members can identify the "man in the ditch" in their daily lives? Our sermons about serving impress and motivate people, but they become impotent when people cannot find a consistent context in which to practice them. No wonder Christians feel so alone and disconnected, even when surrounded by other believers. They have no partners! Most Christians have never found a group of people to whom they can devote their full attention and care.

The moment I serve you (i.e., "wash your feet"), our relationship moves to a different level: we are no longer just acquaintances, we are now partners. The neighbor you greet on the street is an acquaintance, but the moment you help him cut his grass, you move toward a sense of partnership.

How desperately our church members need a group of people they can serve. At Bethany, serving fellow cell members during their times of hospital stay, bereavement or personal crisis becomes a joy for the cell members whose "partners" need help. No longer is it, "Who will volunteer to go and help?" but "One of my spiritual family members is in crisis, and I must be there for that person!" A cell provides a natural environment in which we can rise to the occasion for others.

I recall a family who had moved to Baton Rouge and attended Bethany for their first month in town. The family had not yet attended a cell meeting when their 17-year-old daughter was stricken with Crohn's Disease and began losing enough blood to die. The hospital called Bethany to inform us that we had been listed as this family's church. Immediately a cell group was assigned to them. For one month as the daughter lay in intensive care, cell members donated blood, cooked meals and cleaned their home. The cell grew very close to the family, and needless to say, when the daughter was released, the family had found a church home!

2. Encouragement
The second principle of partnership that Christ taught to His disciples was the principle of "encouragement." In John 14:1, Jesus'

tone shifted from *serving* to *hope*. When He noticed their obvious disappointment that He was leaving, Jesus said, "Do not let your hearts be troubled." How many Christians do you know with "heart trouble"? Broken families, disappointments, failures, depressing diagnoses of disease can leave even the most staunch Christian downcast. Christ was the Master Encourager. He shifted the disciples' focus toward "heaven" (see v. 2), "answered prayer" (see vv. 13,14) and the "Holy Spirit's arrival" (see v. 26).

When Christians gather as groups, their sights are lifted from the depressing to the exciting. Testimonies are shared of victories...failures are confessed and released...spiritual gifts operate and encourage. So many Christians go through discouraging times without anyone to comfort them, but just seeing the familiar face of a close Christian friend can bring encouragement! A spiritual partnership welds people into a family unit where the members are concerned to "spur one another on toward love and good deeds" (Heb. 10:24).

3. Productivity

The third partnership principle Jesus taught His disciples was that of "productivity." In John 15, Jesus deals with *bearing fruit*: "You did not choose me, but I chose you and appointed you to go and bear fruit—fruit that will last" (v. 16).

After 20 years of pastoral ministry, I have discovered that people produce better in groups than by themselves. If I preach on evangelism, people may evangelize that week or perhaps the next. Then as soon as I preach on a different theme, the congregation changes its focus and moves on to the next emphasis. They no longer evangelize! In groups, however, a consistent momentum of evangelism is maintained by the spiritual goals the group is working toward.

The reason for this increased productivity is that partnerships do not simply add the work of one with the work of another. In partnerships the work increases at an exponential rate. Moses asked, "How could one man chase a thousand, or two put ten thousand to flight?" (Deut. 32:30). The production of two people is not equal to their efforts added together. Instead, their "partnership" causes a multiplication. Some people refer to this multiplication phenomena as *synergy* (the sum of the whole is greater than the sum of the parts).

People in relational groups tend to set goals and pool their energies to accomplish those goals. NASA has a famous test in which individuals are given a list of 15 items on a sheet of paper (string, an FM radio, a life raft and other objects). The astronauts are then told that they are marooned on the moon about 200 miles from a mother ship. They must cross the terrain on foot, carrying only some of the items with them. The goal of the test is to have each person list the items in numerical order according to priority. After answering the problem, each individual is assigned to a team and together the team solves the problem as a group. Consistently, the score they corporately produce is 35 to 40 percent higher than their individual scores!

A hilarious illustration of the futility and lack of productivity that results from refusing to partner with others is illustrated in the following story taken from Dr. John Maxwell's book *Developing the Leader Within You*:

> People who are placed in leadership positions, but attempt to do it all alone, will someday come to the same conclusion as the brick layer who tried to move five hundred pounds of bricks from the top of a four-story building to the sidewalk below. His problem was that he tried to do it alone. On an insurance claim form, he explained what happened: "It would have taken too long to carry the bricks down by hand, so I decided to put them in a barrel and lower them by a pulley which I had fastened to the top of the building. After tying the rope securely at the ground level, I then went up to the top of the building. I fastened the rope around the barrel, loaded it with the bricks, and swung it out over the sidewalk for the descent.
>
> "Then I went down to the sidewalk and untied the rope, holding it securely to guide the barrel down slowly.

But, since I weigh only one hundred and forty pounds, the five hundred-pound load jerked me from the ground so fast that I didn't have time to think of letting go of the rope. And as I passed between the second and third floors, I met the barrel coming down. This accounts for the bruises and lacerations on my upper body.

"I held tightly to the rope until I reached the top, where my hand become jammed in the pulley. This accounts for my broken thumb. At the same time, however, the barrel hit the sidewalk with a bang and the bottom fell out. With the weight of the bricks gone, the barrel weighed only about forty pounds. Thus, my one hundred forty-pound body began a swift descent, and I met the empty barrel coming up. This accounts for my broken ankle.

"Slowed only slightly, I continued the descent and landed on the pile of bricks. This accounts for my sprained back and broken collar bone.

"At this point, I lost my presence of mind completely and let go of the rope. And the empty barrel came crashing down on me. This accounts for my head injuries.

"As for the last question on the form, 'What would you do if the same situation arose again?' please be advised that I am finished trying to do the job alone."[1]

4. Protecting

The fourth principle of partnership is found in John 16. Christ's attention turns from *serving*, *encouraging* and *producing* to "protecting." He is concerned that His disciples "should not be offended" (John 16:1, *KJV*). The word "offended" comes from the Greek word *scandalon*, which means a "trap stick."

Many of us as kids had a little cardboard box which we propped up with a stick that had a string tied around it. We dropped bread crumbs leading to the box and put a piece of bread inside, hoping that some innocent bird would follow the crumbs into the box so we could pull the string from our hiding place. The "trap stick" is the *scandalon*.

Christ could see the potential for His disciples to be tricked into a spiritual trap. Everyone has blind spots, areas of temptation that we do not see without the discernment of others. You

> *A spiritual family, or cell group, provides a safe place for people to be open and transparent at the first hint of temptation: this is "preventive maintenance," not "damage control."*

or I could be following "bread crumbs" right now and not even know it! The principle of accountability has been the bedrock basis of the Promise Keepers movement and thousands of men have now found security in utter transparency. These men have learned that to be in weekly accountability groups keeps the "high thoughts" of temptation from becoming the "strongholds" of sinful actions.

Spiritual partnerships afford "protection." In larger churches, Christians are often tempted, tripped up and backslidden for weeks or months before anyone even notices! To compound their condition, the enemy whispers to them, "No one has even checked on you since you fell away...they never loved you in the first place."

A spiritual family, or cell group, provides a safe place for people to be open and transparent at the first hint of temptation: this is "preventive maintenance," not "damage control." We recognized the benefit of this principle in 1996 during a discussion among the Bethany staff regarding how many "church family" divorces we had counseled that year. To our amazement, we could only find one family involved in our cells that had actually divorced! That is one too many, but nowhere near the amount we saw before the cells were in place. The cells have actually formed a much stronger protective wall around tender, vulnerable believers.

These first four partnership principles can be illustrated well by the classic V formation in which a flock of geese fly. Why don't they fly alone? First, because they can rotate turns at the lead where the wind resistance is the greatest. Geese actually practice "serving" each other! Second, because they can encourage each other. The real reason geese "honk" at each other is to encourage the ones that are struggling and tired! Third, because they are corporately breaking the wind resistance. They have a 71 percent greater flying range when they fly as a group than when they fly alone. They are more productive, reach their goal faster and don't have to work as hard as when they are out there flapping their wings alone! Finally, and most important, they protect each other. Whenever a goose is shot or diseased and falls to the ground, it is accompanied by two other geese who leave the flock and watch it from a distance. If it recovers, they wait together for the next flock flying overhead and join that flock. What would have been a horrible, lonely fall becomes a group victory. If only we had as much sense as geese![2]

5. Praying

The last principle of partnership that Jesus taught was "praying." His high priestly prayer in John 17 is a classic illustration of intercession for partners. Instead of praying for everyone in the world, Jesus asked the Father to protect and prosper His partners.

We cannot effectively pray for everyone. We can, however, easily pray for a small group of believers for whom we are vitally concerned. The term "prayer partners" has taken on new meaning in our cells as cell members end each meeting with personal prayer, take prayer walks around the city together, focus in prayer on one people group and missionary, and pray together in other creative ways.

Jesus said, "If two of you shall agree on earth as touching any thing that they shall ask, it shall be done for them of my

Father which is in heaven. For where two or three are gathered together in my name, there am I in the midst of them" (Matt. 18:19,20, *KJV*): Now that is partnership! We have discovered that believers whose names incessantly showed up on "prayer cards" in the main services have had major breakthroughs when a cell group surrounded them weekly and focused on their chronic needs.

These five principles of partnership give us a solid biblical pattern for relational teams. At Bethany, we do not look at our cells as "meetings," but "partnerships." Heaven knows we don't need another meeting! In a partnership, however, people don't "decide" to attend the "meeting" each week if it was good last week...they go to see their partners. The result of this attitude toward the church is powerful, effective and efficient.

"VOLUNTEERISM" OR "SHARED RESPONSIBILITY"?

Once the congregation has discovered the *power* of partnership, it is ready for the next step: the *work* of partnership. Not only is each cell going to have a task, but it will also have a share in the larger tasks of the whole church. This principle of "shared work" is beautifully illustrated in the third chapter of Nehemiah. Nehemiah 3 does not cover any great theological truths, only an account of who rebuilt the different sections of the wall of Jerusalem: family by family, section by section and gate by gate. Instead of insisting ALL of the workers try to build on ALL of the wall, Nehemiah assigned each family a "bite-sized" section of the wall to complete. In this way, no one family carried too much or too little. The work was evident to all and each family was personally fulfilled by completing its assigned "section."

Solomon employed the "shared responsibility" principle when he assigned one tribe each month to bring the daily provisions to Jerusalem (see 1 Kings 4:7). That tribe worked hard 1 month and then was off for 11 months. This rotating, "shared responsibility," kept the service in the house of the Lord special and exciting. Our church has now entered into this kind of rotating partnership.

Bethany has 7 "Districts" comprised of 14 "Zones." Each of the 14 Zones is assigned to minister for 1 week in the house of the Lord. Zone members perform all the service of ushering, greeting, parking, altar work, nursery work, intercession and any other work during the services that week. Then, they are "off" for the next 13 weeks as other Zones take their place. Of course, we have a core of faithful "lifers" who have served in those positions for years and could not imagine not serving every week in that capacity! We use each Zone to "wrap around" our core of lifers and give them ample fresh recruits each week. The result? No one is burned out: the work proceeds forward with joy as everyone gets their "turn" at serving.

Elim Church had a powerful impact on our pastors in 1993 when we sent all of them to San Salvador, El Salvador, to see this dynamic church of almost 50,000 members and 4,500 cell groups. Eager cell members at Elim Church rush to a bulletin board each Sunday to see if it is their turn to serve as deacons, ushers or other workers in the following week! They meet annually as an entire congregation in the largest city stadium. More than 1,000 buses bring in the massive congregation, each bus rented by a section of cells. Every aspect of the meeting flows flawlessly as Zones perform their service.

Every part of a body must move and function or the parts that don't will atrophy. Our "flabby" churches are often filled with observers who watch the 15 percent who do everything serve them week after week. "Partnership" means "partners in the same ship"! By sharing the responsibility, we are "toning up" the Body, giving every member an outlet in which to serve.

The concept of "shared responsibility" came to me more than ever when I received a call one day from the late Dr. Lester Sumrall. His ministry owns a cargo ship named the "Spirit," which regularly docks and reloads for its many worldwide journeys of mercy at the ports along the Gulf of Mexico. His request was for us to host the ship for three months in the Baton Rouge port, ministering spiritually to the 70 crew members! A task such as that before we had "cells" would have been a nightmare, as initial enthusiasm would have turned into neglect and an apology about "doing the best we could."

Instead, in a flash our staff assigned each of the 70 crew members to a section of cells and requested that they go out to the boat and meet their "crewperson." The cell members began bringing their "assigned person" to their cell meetings. During the 90 days, the cells even got involved in remodeling the refrigeration and many other systems of the ship! After three months in port, Dr. Sumrall sent me a fax saying that they had never been so well pastored anywhere they had been, and I had only spent 10 minutes in organization.

This is the beauty of "shared responsibility." Everyone does a little bit of a huge job and the workload is spread across the "many hands that make quick work." I told Dr. Sumrall that I could not take credit for the effort, hardly even knowing that the work was going on! Now, ANY job Bethany undertakes, from outreaches to working at church services, must be one that can be shared by the cells or we do not undertake it.

PASTORAL PARTNERSHIP

I once read the story of a frantic mother who lost her child in a massive wheat field. Many people hunted for hours and days individually, trying to find the child. Finally, everyone involved in the search gathered together and walked the fields shoulder to shoulder, acre by acre, until the little girl's lifeless body was discovered. If only those in charge had begun the search partnering together, the child probably would have been spared. In the same way partnership preserves those who might otherwise go unnoticed in the church.

Just as an individual cell discovers partnership and those cells partner in the work of the church, the pastoral staff partners to pastor the entire flock. Some members will not be in cells, so we have chosen to have a District approach to pastoral care. People who are not in cell groups are cared for by the pastor of the District where they live. The goal is that the "net" be unbroken, and that no one "fall through the cracks."

The "District" concept simply means that a pastor or group of pastors is responsible for certain zip codes. State and city governments have found this to be the best way to care for their citizens. Churches should follow the same pattern. For Bethany, the District concept is the "front door" of the church. As I will explain shortly, members are not locked into a District just because they live there. However, for purposes of follow-up and assimilation, we have found the District concept to be the most effective.

People saved at the altar in one of our services go directly into our "Touch Center" building and a District Office which oversees their residence zip codes. The exception to this would be if any of these people were brought to church by members who have been attempting to win them to Christ and already have a relationship with them. In those instances, the new believer would be directed to that member's District where his or her follow-up process would begin. The "District" is the initial gateway for new people who have few or no relationships within the church.

The "Zone pastor" (one of several within a "District") is also responsible for those church members who are not in a cell but whose zip codes are within their Zones. The "Zone pastor" does the counseling, pastoral care and hospital care for an assigned member in tandem with a cell that is also encouraged to reach out and bond to that member. In this way, no one is "lost." New converts and non-cell members are immediately directed to the right pastors.

Within each Zone and District, homogeneous cells (affinity and relationally based rather than geographically based) may form that bring in members from other Zones or Districts (more about this subject in chapter 8). Pastors do not jealously guard their "lines," but allow believers the freedom of movement they need to find the group that best fits them.

Our first three years of cell ministry were strictly geographic. However, now that our structure is in place, we have the flexibility of movement. Our concern is that every single one of our people is pastored well and that we know who is responsible for them in case of a crisis, not to know who has the "most" or "least." Marriages and funerals are also performed by the Zone pastor in that geographical area unless the person or family has a particular affinity to a different staff pastor. "Accountability and flexibility" are the goal, and the pastors partner together to make it happen.

God is strengthening the net. His heart is that He would be able to send a "multitude of fish" to our boats without them "beginning to sink." The key is *partnership*: "And they beckoned unto their *partners*, which were in the other ship, that they should come and help them" (Luke 5:7, KJV, italics added). Are we ready for that massive harvest? The interconnecting web of relationships in a cell forms the "grid" that can hold the "fish" in the net. Having laid the foundation of pastoral care for them, let's talk about how to bring them in!

Notes

1. John C. Maxwell, *Developing the Leader Within You* (Nashville: Thomas Nelson Publishers, 1993), pp. 113-114.
2. John C. Maxwell, *Developing the Leaders Around You* (Nashville: Thomas Nelson Publishers, 1995), pp. 8-9.

EVANGELISM
IN THE
CELL CHURCH

What pastor doesn't have a burning passion to see unsaved people come to church, demonstrate true repentance, grow in grace
and become leaders themselves? Pastors flash impressive numbers
of "decisions" in response to the latest approach to the lost, however, the most ambitious methods of "follow-up" generally only
conserve at best between 2 and 5 percent of their evangelistic
efforts. As the pastor of an aggressive, growing American church,
I confess that I too have tried many methods to reach the lost.

Bethany's approaches have included hosting a "Summer of
Harvest" in which about 1,500 people responded during one summer to a weekly Saturday morning door-to-door neighborhood
blitz; celebrating "Big Days" in which the lost were strategically
invited to a service; purchasing prime-time television spots to
show specials on local networks with counselors manning phone

lines; and presenting special dramas and concerts including performances with Christian weight lifters. All of these evangelistic efforts were productive, but the sad reality is that they lacked consistency. Every new effort required my personal "push," momentum and execution. The congregation seemed to mirror that pattern: a swell of enthusiasm was followed by a lull of relaxation.

A show of hands in cell conferences typically reveals that approximately 75 percent of believers were born again, not by visiting a service, but because they developed a personal relationship with a believer! The question then becomes, Why are we spending the vast majority of our time with "event" evangelism when people are most affected by one-on-one relationships? Within the answer to that simple question lies the beauty of cell evangelism.

BRIDGING THE GAP OF UNBELIEF THROUGH EDIFIED CELLS

Admittedly, until I heard about the evangelistic emphasis of the cells in El Salvador, I had no interest in cells. On a trip to Mexico, I was told of a large church in San Salvador that held two meetings per week: one for "edification" (planning and edifying), usually held on a Tuesday night, and one for "evangelism" held on Saturday night. Members were all asked on Tuesday to name the unsaved people they would bring on Saturday. Then on Saturday night, the message and method of the meeting catered to the lost, and relationships were formed that either resulted in an immediate conversion or a *bridge-building* relationship. The following Tuesday, that past Saturday's "evangelism" meeting was evaluated and new plans were made for the following Saturday. Roles were assigned for prayer, worship, hospitality and other needed functions.

I caught the vision, believing that in America the same strategy would be effective. However, I felt that instead of twice weekly, a once-a-week meeting could vary its format in the same way, planning and evangelizing on alternate weeks. For the past four years, our cells at Bethany have met in this way. The first week's "planning and edification" gathering centers around meeting the needs of believers, doing spiritual warfare, releasing spiritual gifts and teaching on spiritual maturity. The following week's lesson centers on a "felt need" topic (divorce, loneliness, depression, parenting, etc.), and the cell members invite their unsaved friends who may fall into that category.

This alternating strategy has worked well for Bethany, with almost 5,000 conversions in that four-year period. Frustrations in follow-up, assimilation and preserving the fruit have driven us to develop our present structure of leadership and discipleship training.

Each cell group sets up a three-by-four "white board" in a chair at the edification meeting. The names of the targeted "three most likely" candidates for salvation are listed on the board. The group then spends time praying over those names and doing spiritual warfare for the following week's evangelism meeting. The chart keeps the group continually focused on unsaved souls. When someone who is listed on the chart becomes a believer, that person's name is removed and another is added.

Obviously, the board is not set up on the night evangelism takes place. In fact, if an unbeliever happens to show up at an edification-type meeting, the group is introduced to the person as a "friend." "Friend" is a code word indicating that the newcomer is unsaved, and the meeting shifts to a "seeker sensitive" evangelistic format! I've watched cell leaders masterfully shift a meeting from praise, worship, spiritual warfare, etc., to a simple topical discussion the moment an unbeliever enters an "edification" meeting.

Our church has geared its primary evangelistic visibility in the city toward small groups. Large interstate billboards show "Hope within reach...a Lifeline Touch Group." Yard signs are placed in front of the host homes that say, "Lifeline Touch Group meets here...we're here for you." A "Tonight" sign is hung on the night of the cell meeting. *Lifeline*, our daily 2-minute television program on all three network affiliates, ends with a 30-second commercial inviting viewers to call for the Touch Group nearest their home.

FOUR BASIC PRINCIPLES OF EVANGELISM

The Latin American city of Bogota, Colombia, has provided us with the second great evangelism strategy of cells: the "Principle of Twelve." This principle will be fully explained in chapter 8, but we can summarize it here by saying that all cell members receive the vision to have their own cells of 12 members and to develop those 12 cell members into cell leaders. At the time of this writing, some in Bogota have grown from 5 to 400 cells in only two years!

By studying the world's greatest cell churches I have discovered four basic principles of evangelism that are common to all: *purpose, partnership, prayer* and *penetration.* These four principles must be taught again and again to every cell member to help maintain a "charge" of evangelism that does not wax and wane.

The four principles are typified in the characteristics of four little animals mentioned in Proverbs 30:24-28. These four animals are "small, yet are exceedingly wise." "He who wins souls is wise" (11:30), and these little creatures buried in the book of Proverbs demonstrate soul-winning wisdom. The first and most important principle is the focus of "purpose."

THE PAST, THE PICKLE, THE PURPOSE

I recall standing in front of the 1:00 P.M. Sunday service at Dr. Yonggi Cho's Yoido Full Gospel Church in Seoul, Korea. I was preaching to an estimated 50,000 people in what was only one of seven Sunday services packed into the main sanctuary, seating 25,000 people with auxiliary chapels seating another 25,000.

I thought of how the Koreans have literally rebuilt their country from devastation in the mid 1950s to one of the world's top industrial powers. I preached that day on the "ant," thinking of how busy and resourceful the Koreans have become in order to achieve their goals: "Ants are creatures of little strength, yet they store up their food in the summer" (30:25). The ant's drive, purpose and resourcefulness is legendary.

I once heard that while Ghengis Khan was hiding in a barn following a defeat in battle, his life was impacted by watching an ant. The ant, which was carrying a heavy load, attempted to climb over a board 71 times (!), tumbling off with every attempt. But on the seventy-second try, the ant succeeded. Ghengis Khan decided that if an ant could have that much perseverance and make it, so could he. He went back and led his troops to a great victory!

The ant is motivated to store up food during the summer months. Every day the ant leaves its home, desperately looking for food before the winter begins. If these little creatures happen to smell the food of an innocent picnicker, they will attack even though their human enemies outweigh them by hundreds of pounds! Ants know they have a limited time to gather in the harvest, and that the winter will be cold, wet and fruitless. Like the ant, Christians must have a "purpose" in winning souls. Without purpose their motivation will wane.

The great Elim Church in El Salvador recognizes almost 50,000 members and has taught its cell members the following "Fivefold Purpose Statement" which is the vision of evangelism for the church:

1. **I have a purpose.** I am not just *bumping along* through life with no direction or reason for existence.
2. **My purpose is winning souls.** This is my highest and ultimate calling on earth.
3. **I fulfill my purpose best in a group.** I maximize my potential when in partnership.
4. **I will never be satisfied until I fulfill my purpose.** No hobbies, jobs or relationships can bring me inward satisfaction like winning the lost.
5. **I have no promise of tomorrow.** I must work while I have the chance because I don't know how long I have left to reach the lost.

These five potent statements of *purpose* have become the heartbeat of every believer in that powerful local church in El Salvador. The apostle Paul's Damascus experience records the

> *Believers in American churches need to wake up each morning with more purpose than paying bills and eating sausage biscuits at McDonald's!*

same purposeful dynamic: "But arise, and stand on your feet; for this *purpose* I have appeared to you...to open their eyes so that they may turn from darkness to light and from the dominion of Satan to God, in order that they may receive forgiveness of sins and an inheritance among those who have been sanctified by faith in Me" (Acts 26:16,18, *NASB*, italics added). Believers in American churches need to wake up each morning with more purpose than paying bills and eating sausage biscuits at McDonald's!

Incidentally, my own sense of purpose was once challenged with a trip to McDonald's! I drove around the back of the restaurant to pick up my Big Mac at the side window. Determined to eat on the way, I carefully unwrapped my burger and pulled out into traffic. Suddenly, after the first bite, a large pickle (baptized in mustard) dropped onto my lap. I could not help being distracted by it and reached for a napkin to wipe it from my clean trousers. The momentary, downward glance caused my car to drift into the other lane, and when I looked up, an 18 wheeler was bearing down upon me!

I quickly swerved back into the correct lane and with a palpitating heart heard the Lord say, "What's happening through the windshield is far more important than what is happening in your lap!" In other words, the pickle seemed important, but my forward vision was critical. Many of us focus on the insignificant, the meaningless and the irrelevant while the bigger vision goes neglected! Some focus on the **past** (the rearview mirror), some focus on the **pickle** (the present details), but Paul focused on the **purpose** (the winning of eternal souls). He called this foundational principle the "heavenly vision":

"Consequently, King Agrippa, I did not prove disobedient to the *heavenly vision*, but kept declaring both to those of Damascus first, and also at Jerusalem and then throughout all the region of Judea, and even to the Gentiles, that they should repent and turn to God, performing deeds appropriate to repentance" (Acts 26:19,20, *NASB*, italics added).

Christians with purpose have "vision," and, like the ant, enter each day with a sense of urgency and motivation to "store up their food in the summer" (Prov. 30:25).

The inward fire of the "ant" must be coupled with the wisdom of the second animal, the badger, which gains its strength from its associations: "The rock badgers are a feeble folk, yet they make their houses in the crags [rocks]" (v. 26, *NKJV*). The wisdom of the badger brings us to the application of a second great truth for cell group evangelism: the "Principle of Partnership."

PURPOSEFUL PARTNERSHIPS PROMOTE PROTECTION

We discussed Jesus' teaching on partnership in detail in chapter 3. The badger's wisdom, however, sheds additional light on productive group evangelism. The badger is a shy little animal that retreats quickly into the safety of huge boulders when threatened. The badger's strength lies not in its "abilities," but in its "associations." Permit me to illustrate: If I were lying on the beach and a 280-pound bully kicked sand into my face, chances are I would act as if I did not notice his assault! But, if I had Evander Holyfield and Reggie White standing on either side of me, I might be tempted to ask the bully, "Do you have a problem, or are you looking for one?" My strength is not necessarily in my ability, but in my associations!

Partnership brings confidence: "I fulfill my purpose best in a group." The group is a friendly, gospel environment where unbelievers can be introduced to "normal" Christian people and presented with the gospel by relationship. Such an environment immediately dispels the myth that "Christians have no friends," or that all Christians are weird, boring "geeks." Nonbelievers experience a caring, serious atmosphere where their deepest needs can be discussed and lovingly ministered to.

Christians are bolder about inviting the unsaved to a home than to a church. Once community has formed among the cell members, they trust each other implicitly to have a powerful gospel impact on the family members, coworkers and neighbors they protect so carefully.

In such a trusting environment, timid "badgers" disappear into the safety of their mature, cell-member "boulders." They don't have to go out knocking on doors and presenting gospel surveys. Instead, they simply invite unbelievers to meet with their friends.

Many of our evangelistic cell meetings are "eating meetings." A barbecue, a "crawfish boil" (inedible by all of you living outside of Louisiana), and other food events break down the defenses and open wide doors into even the most reprobate hearts. Timid "badgers" get excited about having a place where their unsaved family and friends will be totally blown away with the love of genuine Christianity. The group discussions that include an *icebreaker, cell lesson* and *application* are all geared toward unbelievers to foster a perfectly safe environment!

The partnership principle of evangelism also means that the 12 cell members will brainstorm together for outreach events. One of our cells distributed Christmas baskets to the apartment complex where it met and had 12 decisions for Christ in one evening. Another group collected school supplies to sponsor a school supply giveaway for the entire neighborhood. One hundred twenty-six people showed up at the cell and many were saved! GREAT IDEAS come out of partnership, and formerly sporadic, unfruitful believers suddenly become continuously motivated.

The third animal Proverbs 30 mentions is the locust. In the air, millions of locusts can almost block out the sun's light. They control the atmosphere! Joel describes the great "locust army" as a side-by-side army that "rush on the city, [and] run on the wall" (Joel 2:9, *NASB*). What a perfect illustration of an unconventional army, highly focused and demonstrating the third principle of cell evangelism: the "Principle of Prayer."

PRAYER: BREAKING DOWN SPIRITUAL RESISTANCE

The breaking down of spiritual resistance is vital to soul winning. Jesus said that Paul's vision would become a reality when he "turn[ed] them from darkness to light, and from the power of Satan to God" (Acts 26:18). Much has been written about spiritual warfare, but the reality is that cell groups must first **generate revival** and then **contain** revival.

The major cell churches of the world have released millions of hours of focused spiritual warfare for the lost. Believers within a cell find their dreams for evangelism being fulfilled when they join rank in prayer and fasting for the lost.

One of my dearest friends in ministry is our former youth pastor, Ted Haggard, pastor of New Life Church in Colorado Springs, Colorado. When Ted arrived in Colorado Springs in 1985, there were at best only a handful of significant churches in the city. Pastors were discouraged, churches were not impacting the culture and more than 200 witchcraft covens openly owned businesses.

Ted and his small nucleus of intercessors met in the basement of his home and began doing "on site with insight" spiritual warfare around those diabolic businesses. They even prayed from the top of Cheyenne Mountain where witchcraft sacrifices are conducted, breaking those curses of darkness over the city. (See Ted's great book *Primary Purpose* published by Creation House for more details). The results have been amazing.

In just 12 short years, Ted has planted a church with 6,000 attending on Sunday mornings. Someone previously termed Colorado Springs a "graveyard of churches," but in the last few years, more than 100 Christian ministries from all across America have moved into that city. Today, Colorado Springs is often referred to as the "Wheaton of the West"! Prayer has united the pastors, caused the churches to simultaneously grow with conversion growth and challenged the world for missions through the great A.D. 2000 Movement.

The results of this kind of spiritual discipline throughout the world are compelling. For example, in Bogota, each cell member completes a liquids only fast for the first 3 days of each month and then a weekly 1-day fast (until the evening meal). As a group, cell members fast for 10 consecutive days once each year and also participate in an annual 40-day fast that lasts each day until the evening meal! This commitment to fasting and prayer is literally breaking down the demonic strongholds over Bogota, and geographical regions of that city have already been "conquered" spiritually!

The same kind of attention is given to prayer and fasting in Korea. Days begin in Seoul with thousands of early morning prayer meetings happening in practically every church. Most denominations have large "prayer mountain" facilities where members go to pray and fast. Individuals and cell groups go to the prayer mountains and fast for up to 40 days, praying all day and night in little prayer grottoes barely five feet long, three feet wide and four feet high. Is it any wonder that the largest congregations in all the major denominations are in Seoul?

In the same way, we have challenged every cell member at Bethany to evangelize first by prayer and fasting. One of our cell leaders recently testified that his cell had not multiplied in more than 18 months. Having tried all the methods of cell evangelism, the group was still unsuccessful. During the first 3 months of 1997, the group began to pray and fast. The result: seven new believers were all born again in the cell meetings! Our studies of Bethany cells have consistently shown that groups that focus on prayer and fasting repeatedly win souls and multiply while those that don't stagnate and often disappear.

In February of 1996, our cell groups had four successive weekends of prayerwalks. The first weekend, the members each walked around various public schools. Some of the principals had been alerted to the prayerwalk and even invited the members to walk the halls and pray over the school lockers. Shortly afterward, the school board called and asked to have its annual convocation with 5,000 teachers at our church. The meeting was broadcast live for four hours over the local network television stations! We are now going in and renovating public schools each month. God is giving mighty favor—a direct result of prayer.

The second weekend we spent walking around all 500 churches in the city, praying for blessing. Individual cell members even attended these churches on Sunday morning and informed the pastors of their love and prayers. Some of our members were invited to teach on prayer in their Sunday Schools!

On the third weekend our cell members walked around the "high places" of Baton Rouge: abortion clinics, gambling casinos, palm reading establishments, pornographic bookstores and other places where demonic strongholds exist. Many people did not get out of their cars at the establishments, but prayed as groups within their cars.

During the final weekend, cell members walked around the government, police, fire, school board and all community governmental buildings. We cried out to God asking for revival and open doors among elected officials. When believers develop a sense of *purpose* and *partnership*, they produce effective "prayer." The results of this prayer will be described in the last principle of evangelism in cells, typified by the lizard: the "Principle of Penetration."

PENETRATING DARKNESS WITH PURPOSE, PARTNERSHIP AND PRAYER

Have you ever had a visit from an uninvited lizard? Most likely, it found a tiny hole in your masonry or wall, stuck its pointed little head inside, and may have spent two weeks soaking up the air conditioning before you discovered it! The lizard has no concern for status or position: one little hole, and it's in. "The lizard you may grasp with the hands, yet it is in kings' palaces" (Prov. 30:28, *NASB*). Just as the lizard, when we begin to focus on the Great Commission as a united Body, prayerfully seeking a way to bring Christ's love into the palaces and projects of the world, God will make a way.

God is penetrating the darkness worldwide through cell evangelism. In November 1995 at our annual Missions Convention, Pastor Donald Matheny of the Nairobi Lighthouse Church in Nairobi, Kenya, presented a powerful picture of the way the Lord is using cell evangelism to change Africa. This great church had 1,500 members when its leaders first came to Bethany in June of 1994 to study our cells.

In August 1994, Nairobi Lighthouse launched its cells, and by August 1997 (just three years later) its 450 cell groups were winning a monthly average of 350 people to the Lord *in cells*. The church has now grown to more than 3,500 members, meeting in a large outdoor stadium on Sunday morning, and has surpassed Bethany in vision and soul-winning motivation.

Pastor Matheny's message to us at our annual Missions Convention was based on Luke 5: "And He got into one of the boats....And He sat down" (v. 3, *NASB*). Pastor Matheny said that his cell groups had learned the secret of cell evangelism from studying the way Christ responded to Peter's indifference. Peter was simply "washing his nets," unmotivated to hear Christ preach on the beach. Rather than waiting for Peter to join Him, Christ went to Peter and asked permission to enter his boat. Peter's "boat," he explained, was his "world." Everything in his life revolved around that "boat." The secret to evangelism, he pointed out, is to enter a person's "boat" and "sit down."

Cell members from Nairobi Lighthouse offer to empty the garbage for people living in surrounding housing developments, informing residents that cell members will be coming by each Sunday evening and instructing people to leave their garbage on the curb for pickup. Broken down city services have allowed piles of garbage to accumulate, but these serving Christians enter the world of the lost as they load the smelly refuse on to wheelbarrows and cart it away. In one housing development, 30 residents attended the first cell meeting after a few weeks of watching cell members remove garbage for them!

Traditional evangelism is primarily an invitation to come and get into "our boats." Cell evangelism, however, is discovering the interest and need of the unbeliever and entering that person's world. Believers are challenged to be "lizards" by penetrating the world in which the unbeliever is most secure. Every interest an unsaved person expresses (outside of a sinful interest) is seen as a tiny hole in the stronghold of that life. The lizard aggressively penetrates that world, serving and ministering in every way possible.

Many of our groups have penetrated the world of international students at our local state university, inviting them to cell groups for "meals." When the international students enter the cell meeting, they find their flag hanging on the wall, a seven-course meal of their native food and music from their homeland playing on the stereo! Their national map lies on the coffee table where they all gather for fellowship after dinner. Cell members encourage relationship by asking the students questions about their culture and religion. The mood is one of cultural exchange. The lizards are going in! Having penetrated their world, lizards are often able to start a homogeneous cell on campus with these students!

The campus is just one of the many places Bethany's lizards have found an opening. The "lizard...is in kings' palaces"...and governors' mansions. During a recent churchwide 21-day fast, my wife and I both sensed that our governor's mansion would be opened to the gospel. Within 10 days, the governor phoned my office after seeing our two-minute *Lifeline* program on television. He asked me to come and teach the historical background of the Bible to himself and 10 of his personal staff!

That teaching has now evolved into a weekly Bible study and

prayer session which has, as of this writing, continued for nine months. Every Wednesday, we gather around the governor's breakfast table to pray after our study. This meeting has true "cell group" dynamics, and the group seems to have learned a lot about the Bible in the meantime. God opened the door, and the lizard has penetrated the mansion!

Cell members must learn to *penetrate*. They must be motivated to use the cell group as the means for leading unsaved friends and relatives to Christ, believing that: "I am a missionary to America. I am in an evangelistic enterprise, and my cell will be the means by which I will reach the lost." The cell is the most powerful medium of gospel witness in America today.

When believers catch the vision for cells, an internal explosion occurs! Something I call, "the anointing to multiply" takes over, and they become incredibly innovative and involved. *Purpose, partnership, prayer* and *penetration* are the keys that unlock the creative juices in believers and the minds of unbelievers. The result is "multiplication." Let's look at this "multiplication anointing" and see how it has helped our cells to maintain a vision for growth!

BE FRUITFUL AND MULTIPLY

I am writing this chapter, having just attended the 1997 Church Growth Conference hosted by Dr. Yonggi Cho in Seoul, Korea. No stranger to any pastor worldwide, Dr. Cho's Yoido Full Gospel Church is by far the largest in the world. His cell leaders, primarily women, have set incredible goals and harvested enormous crops of evangelistic fruit.

A leader in Dr. Cho's church received an award for winning 365 *families* to the Lord in one year...one family for every day of that year! As we all know, an abundance of fruit such as that is almost unheard of in our American culture. And yet, we are *all* called to this kind of fruitfulness.

Multiplication is a biblical principle. In Genesis 1:28, the Lord's first command to His human creation was, "Be fruitful, and multiply, and replenish the earth, and subdue it" (*KJV*). We not only see the result of this mandate in Genesis 1, but we also find it in Exodus 1:7: "And the children of Israel were fruitful, and increased abundantly, and multiplied, and waxed exceeding mighty" (*KJV*). It seems that "the more [the Egyptians] afflicted them, the more they multiplied and grew" (Exod. 1:12, *KJV*).

Satan fears our multiplication. He is perfectly content to have us warm the church pews and stare at each other week after

> *Nothing incites spiritual warfare more than when believers focus together on the lost! Fortunately, when the Body is united, warfare only causes a greater multiplication to occur.*

week while our cities degenerate into war zones and our youth shoot each other for a pair of tennis shoes. But he becomes incensed when we develop vision and strategy to place a gospel "lighthouse" on every street and in every neighborhood within our region. Nothing incites spiritual warfare more than when believers focus together on the lost! Fortunately, when the Body is united, warfare only causes a greater multiplication to occur.

The Early Church experienced this multiplication principle at work and saw that the "word of God increased; and the number of the disciples multiplied in Jerusalem greatly" (Acts 6:7, *KJV*). Rapid, anointed multiplication took place as "daily in the temple, and in every house, they ceased not to teach and preach Jesus Christ" (5:42, *KJV*). Public events and home cell meetings brought a dynamic rhythm that fed multiplied thousands into the kingdom of God! What is this principle of multiplication and how do we release it?

STAGES OF CELL MULTIPLICATION

We'll begin with a quick look at the biology of human cells, comparing their multiplication process to that of spiritual cells. In both cases, certain elements must be in place for the cell to move to the next level and to finally become "two cells."

What I am about to describe to you is "traditional cell multiplication," the process by which 1 cell grows from roughly 5 to 15 members and births 2 different cells. This process has worked well at Bethany for the last four years, even though now we have discovered that multiplication can happen almost exponentially through the "Principle of Twelve" (discussed in detail in chapter 8). "Traditional multiplication" is the type practiced by most cell churches around the world, and a good working description of the process will prove very helpful for you here.

Stage One: Learning
The first stage is the stage of "learning." In a biological cell, cell multiplication begins when the chromosomes start "pairing up" rather than floating alone inside the cell.

This "pairing" is actually "partnership," the process by which believers get more intimately acquainted and develop bonds. I call this stage "learning" because in this first month or two of a cell meeting, a lot of surface-level exchange occurs among the members: background stories, personal testimonies and other sharing. Everything is "fun" in these first few meetings as the new group evolves. The anticipation of the cell's future and the benefits it will provide stimulates a lot of interest.

During this learning stage of cell development, we emphasize the "fellowship" (light snacks and drinks served for the first 20 minutes) and "icebreaker" portions of the meeting. Food is very important at the first of every meeting! Everyone can contribute by bringing chips or cookies or beverages. Eating together is a safe way to create intimacy. Someone has said that even a 300-pound man can hide behind a coffee cup!

Gradually the meeting transitions to a fellowship time when the group sits around discussing an "icebreaker." The icebreaker is a fun, nonthreatening question that anyone can answer easily: What is a funny dream you have had all of your life? or What kind of car did you drive when you first got your license? The time spent discussing the icebreaker should never be deeply serious, only light and fun. As the group members grow deeper in their understanding of each other, the icebreaker times can trim down to a comfortable 15 minutes. The "learning" stage comes to a close after a few weeks and the next stage happens almost imperceptibly.

Stage Two: Loving

The second stage the group enters is what we call the "loving" stage. In a biological cell, the paired chromosomes now form a "north-south" axis where they gather together into close proximity.

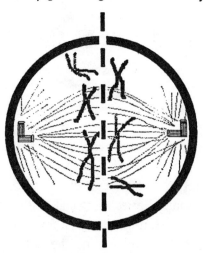

Instead of floating freely in the cytoplasm, the chromosomes are coming into a place of order and association. In a cell group, the "newness" is wearing off and people are beginning to experience conflict. You never know how much you love people until you get close to them! Someone said that you can survive the unsaved, but it's those Christians who will kill you!

Internal alignment may occur within the cell as people's values clash and their commitment levels are reevaluated. The cell almost goes through an "identity crisis" as it has to redefine the question, Why am I a part of this group? This time of introspection is much the same as that which newlyweds experience once the honeymoon is over and the reality of the commitment has become apparent. For Americans, this first level is often especially difficult because we live in a "no commitment" generation. After the second or third month, this stage should also be fulfilled and the cell members are now beginning to move to the third stage.

Stage Three: Linking
The group emerges stronger and more committed to achieving its goal of multiplication in stage three. People begin to define their *roles, goals* and *expectations*. Most conflict can be settled, even in a family, with a fresh communication of *roles* and *goals*. Each member begins to play a distinct part in making the cell meetings happen. In a biological cell, the paired chromosomes move from a "north-south" position to an "east-west" position.

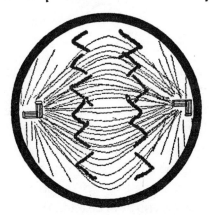

The paired chromosomes have now linked into the position they will be in when they multiply.

A cell group must also have a redefined sense of personal responsibility: "This is MY group, and without my help and participation this cell will not succeed." Now, the group members have ownership: Some lead music, some help with hospitality, some express an interest in intercession for the group, but all play a part. The period of internal struggling and determining the "pecking order" is essentially over by the time stage three occurs, and the group is now focusing on reaching its objectives. The group is successfully forming a "community."

Stage Four: Launching

Next comes the exciting stage: "launching." In the biological cell, the two ends of the cell "equator" start cleaving and pulling outward.

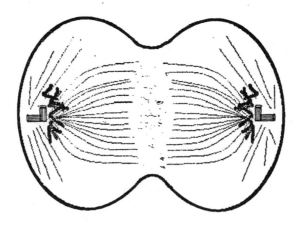

This outward pull ultimately causes the cell to birth into two! Finally, after three or four months of *learning, loving* and *linking,* the cell reaches its most fruitful time. The members love each other and trust each other enough to invite their friends and relatives to come and experience the sense of community that prevails among the members. Bethany's structure includes an "evangelism" lesson every two weeks (borrowing the concept from El Salvador as described in chapter 4).

Though outgrowth has happened in theory during the first three months, it begins in earnest when evangelism becomes a focus. Lots of fun breakthroughs start to happen as the members organize creative outreaches, barbecues and community service projects. During the fourth and fifth month, the group gradually grows. Prayer, intercession and planning become strong and robust in the alternate weeks when evangelism is being planned. The group senses it is approaching the goal of multiplication as its goals have become plans and its plans have become actions.

This fourth (launching) stage can readily be compared to that of a child's growth as it transitions through adolescence. The child moves from the "learning" stage (ages 1 to 5), to the "loving" stage (ages 6 to 9) in which close monitoring and discipline are needed as values clash. By the time the child is 10 to 12, he or she should begin "linking" as the child's role in the family is clearly defined in everything from chores to family traditions. Now, at the onset of adolescence, the young person is ready for a "launching" time: driver's license, dating, athletic events and ministry growth. By age 18, the adolescent is ready for the final, exciting stage: "leaving"!

Stage Five: Leaving

During the fourth stage, a cell intern or "Timothy" has been preparing to handle a new group. This person has led the group at least four times, has an orderly family, has a vision for the new group and has completed leadership training (see chapter 6). What was once an intimidating thought of being a leader has become an exciting door of opportunity. As the group nears multiplication, some reproducing cells actually meet during the regular "discussion" time in separate rooms with the new intern. This preliminary meeting gives the group a feel for the dynamics it will experience when meeting as a separate cell, yet the cell members are still in the *safety* of the mother group.

Multiplying can of itself be an exciting experience. Many groups multiply at a "multiplication party"—a big event attended by the Zone pastor, church members who are not yet in a cell, and even unbelievers. First, the group has an extended time of food and fellowship. Then, the pastor and cell leader sit before the group and explain the vision of what is happening that night. Because the group is being multiplied by the leader and pastor along relational lines, people who have brought others to the group (friends, relatives, acquaintances) will not be separated in the multiplication process. Preserving these relational ties makes the multiplication work smoothly and everyone stays happy!

Multiplication can be tricky, simply because strong relationships have formed during the six-month cycle. Therefore, in order to successfully separate those relationships, the multiplication plan must be discussed by the leadership in advance. It is important that members understand the vision: A cell is like a set of parents who rejoice to see children born and taking their places in leadership.

The Bogota church has a unique solution to the "multiplication blues." As we will see in chapter 8, the "Principle of Twelve" teaches that the new leader will continue to return to the mother cell indefinitely, meeting his/her former leader 30 minutes prior to the meeting and receiving mentoring and encouragement. Thus, the new leader is in a cell where he or she is ministering and also being ministered to. Most traditional cell multiplications do not include continued mentoring for the leaders who are birthed from preexisting cells, but we believe this follow up keeps the Body unified and nurtured.

Whatever the method of multiplication, the focus is the same: to give the group an outlet for producing spiritual "children" who can be raised up to reproduce more spiritual children. In a recent publication, *Natural Church Development: A Guide to Eight Essential Qualities of Healthy Churches* by Christian A. Schwarz, a survey of 1,000 churches in 32 nations revealed eight major church-growth principles. From a database of 4.2 million responses, his conclusion is that the most outstanding principle for church growth is "the multiplication of small groups."[1] This gives us the first "scientific" proof of what the Lord spoke to me in 1993: We in America must change our structure to accommodate the coming world revival. Believers must come into the "one another" relationships of *learning, loving, linking, launching,* and *leaving.*

THE CHURCH OF CHAMPIONS

Secular business publications confirm that one of the eight major tenets of successful American businesses has been to break a large corporation down into smaller, tiny units in which each has a goal, a challenge and a measurable sense of progress.[2] American believers, accustomed to large gatherings, often assume that nothing could possibly happen in a small group of 6 to 15 people. The opposite, however, is true. They develop a camaraderie which, when properly motivated, focuses them on fulfilling the vision of multiplication. Assembling ourselves together at Bethany is no longer a "spectator sport" for which members only come as Sunday observers; they are encouraged to become what the business community calls "champions."

A champion is an individual within a corporation who is free to experiment (within boundaries) with a new idea that might greatly benefit the company. Our cell leaders, section leaders, Zone pastors and District pastors are all free to "open cells." Whether it is by traditional multiplication or homogeneous "cell planting" (see chapter 8), the group knows of no barriers to reaching its goal of planting new cell groups. This is an awesome task, and our members have risen to the challenge with a gusto.

"Be fruitful and multiply" (*KJV*). In one simple sentence, God laid down the pattern for His work. *Learning, loving, linking, launching* and *leaving* become the pattern of multiplication for both human and spiritual cells. If we follow that pattern, growth and multiplication are sure to follow. Our primary goal, therefore, must be to develop leaders who will facilitate that multiplication. Remember: Don't focus on cell *attendance* as much as on leadership development. When leaders are properly trained and motivated, they will bring in the attendance! As someone said, "You can't put a dead hen on live chicks," and neither can you attempt to force people to attend a meeting where the leader has no motivation, vision or passion to multiply.

When Jesus multiplied the loaves and fish, I am sure that each time He pulled off a portion of fish more grew back immediately.

I've seen the same process happen with great leaders: You cannot multiply them fast enough. Within a month or two after multiplication, great leaders already have a "full house" again and they are desperately looking for a new leader. The temptation may be to appoint someone to leadership simply because that person is available. The key, however, is to have leaders who are both "motivated and able."

Let's look at some of the ways we have learned to quickly but thoroughly train cell leaders for the multiplication process.

Notes

1. Christian A. Schwarz, *Natural Church Development: A Guide to Eight Essential Qualities of Healthy Churches* (Barcelona, Spain: ChurchSmart Resources, Inc., 1996), p. 33.
2. Thomas J. Peters and Robert H. Waterman, Jr., *In Search of Excellence: Lessons from America's Best-Run Companies* (New York: Warner Books, 1984), pp. 270-277.

LEADERSHIP DEVELOPMENT IN THE CELL CHURCH

"Bethany World Prayer Center exists as a church to *preach* the gospel to every person, *pastor* believers, *prepare* disciples and *plant* leaders in every nation of the world." So reads our church's purpose statement, and implementing the final objective is the emphasis of this chapter.

I love to preach. For years, I believed successful pastoring was merely praying, preaching and programs. However, my hard work and heavy ministry load brought only limited results. I had hired some wonderful staff members, most of whom had been raised up from our church, and I often appointed leaders who simply became "visible" and impressed me. But I hadn't seen the need to spend my time developing others. I knew I was called and would pay the price to be ready every time people came for services, yet it never dawned on me that training leaders would ultimately benefit our church more than anything else I could do.

As we began to transition to a cell structure, I felt the Lord impressing me to invest as much effort in raising up leaders as preaching. That simple change has brought dramatic results.

THE MOSES MINISTRY MAKEOVER MODEL

Moses had a similar problem of self-focused leadership. He was faithful and conscientious, but drowning without delegation. The responsibility of carrying the ministry alone began to weigh him down and wear him out. Finally, his father-in-law, Jethro, persuaded him to release some of his responsibilities to able people who could supervise groups of 10s, 50s, 100s and 1000s (see Exod. 18:21). Moses' primary role would be to "show them the way to live and the duties they are to perform" (v. 20). In other words, his time spent in training leaders would eventually be time saved. By raising up leaders, Moses would be able to more efficiently oversee the 3 million people he was responsible for leading to the Promised Land and still have time to handle cases that were unsolvable for others.

Similarily, Dr. Yonggi Cho's discovery of the cell structure was the result of a health crisis. One night after baptizing 300 new members, Dr. Cho had so overexerted himself that he had a total physical collapse. His frail physical condition left him unable to stand behind his pulpit for more than 10 minutes weekly to preach to his congregation. He approached his deacons for help to carry out the pastoral duties, but they refused. He in turn offered those duties to the ladies of the church and they agreed to help him (see Dr. Cho's book *Successful Home Cell Groups* which describes this process).[1] Now, all the work of the world's largest church is done through his 25,000 cell leaders.

By now you may be thinking, *I would love to release leaders, but can I trust them? What if they divide my church? What if they offend someone? What if they backslide?* A thousand objections will stand in your way, many of which could parallel those of your marriage partner! All partnerships involve risk, but the secret is in the preparation process. Dr. Cho's excellent teaching on the "Seven Dangers in Cells"[2] has helped to steer Bethany clear of the pitfalls that typify the shoreline of leadership delegation.

In the five years since we started cells, each new leader has been thoroughly trained in these dangers and knows the root thoughts Satan can use to deceive a leader into falling for any one of them. This preventative training has helped to circumvent these seven problems. In fact, I cannot cite ONE example of a cell "disaster," though I am sure they have occurred without my knowledge. That does not preclude them from happening, but suffice it to say that the overall effect of releasing leaders to assist us in ministry has far outweighed any negative damage they may have done.

TRAINED LEADERS
TRANSFORM THE CHURCH

You may ask, "What will I teach them?" Teach them what you know! My leadership training begins with isolating a simple principle of wisdom that I have learned as a pastor and then training my leaders in that principle. The "fivefold ministry" (see Eph. 4:11) exists for the "equipping of the saints for the work of service" (v. 12, *NASB*). Training our members begins with the basic premise that every believer can be a leader. Though their levels of leadership will vary based upon their giftings, all believers can be trained in doctrine (from teachers), caring (from pastors), witnessing (from evangelists), spiritual gifts (from prophets) and training others (from apostles).

As I mentioned earlier, a notable example of the benefit from cell leader training has occurred in our church. One of our original 54 cell leaders was a state worker, supervising seven employees when she began as a cell leader. She completed six months of leadership training and immediately began rising in her department.

Her faithfulness and dedication resulted in her recent appointment as the assistant secretary for the Department of Social Services in Louisiana with 3,300 employees under her supervision and an administrative budget of 400 million dollars! Though this woman is obviously gifted as a leader, her leadership skills were enhanced through her cell leader training, and she now often uses her leadership classes as the basis for teaching the many state supervisors under her authority.

All leadership training begins with providing a place for people to use their gifts and abilities. In the majority of American

> *Lack of involvement breeds apathy, stagnation and resignation from any responsibility in the church. In a cell, however, each member has a place and a gift.*

churches, the most anyone "does" in church is stare at the back of the person's head in front of them. This lack of involvement breeds apathy, stagnation and resignation from any responsibility in the church. In a cell, however, each member has a place and a gift. Paul said, "When you come together, everyone has a hymn, or a word of instruction, a revelation, a tongue or an interpretation" (1 Cor. 14:26). In other words, spiritual gifts are meant to be **used**, not discussed.

A smaller group of loving, caring, supporting Christians provides the perfect environment for those who are just learning to use their spiritual gifts. As long as the "heavy hitters" of the spiritual gifts are present in larger services, the more timid will always give way to watching them minister. Thus, the timid are commonly transformed in the safety of the small group and often blossom into powerful leaders.

In addition to having a "place" to minister (a cell), members must also have the confidence that they have been trained to minister. They may be "motivated," but not "able." Notice the paradigm in the following box designed by Dr. Sandy Kulkin of the Institute for Motivational Living.[3] Employers know that a person must move from "no motivation and no ability" to being "motivated and able." Good employers are not satisfied with employees who stay at a level where they must be told, coached or encouraged to do their jobs. They want to raise their employees to a level where they can delegate a task to them and rest assured that it will be accomplished.

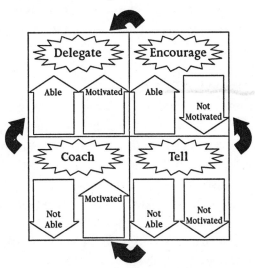

In Bethany's leadership training model, *multiplication* provides the *motivation*, and *a leadership training track* provides the *ability*. Our purpose statement given at the outset of this chapter states how we provide leaders with the confidence that they are equipped to lead.

THE FOUR PURPOSES OF LEADERSHIP TRAINING

It is our conviction, as reflected in our purpose statement, that every leader must be trained to *preach, pastor, prepare* and *plant.* All of the classes, exercises and relationships implemented at Bethany must result in people who can train and release other leaders. The following is a very brief description of how the four levels work. The actual leadership process will be covered in greater detail in chapter 7.

Level One: Trained to Preach

The first level a potential leader must be trained in is in the ability to "preach the gospel to every person." Simple evangelism comes from a desire to win souls. Unless a person overcomes timidity in personal witnessing, he or she will never enter spiritual leadership. Within each cell, every member is encouraged to evangelize by bringing the unsaved to the cell meetings or church services.

Level Two: Trained to Pastor

The second level of training for leaders is the pastoral level. Leaders are taught how to "assimilate" one new believer. The assimilation process may include a visit to that person's home to verify the validity of his or her experience with Christ. The leader may be also be assigned as a "sponsor" to take a new believer through several booklets on true repentance, water baptism or other elementary doctrines. Often the new believer is brought on a spiritual weekend retreat where sin issues are illuminated and frequently resolved.

Level Three: Trained to Teach

The third level is the preparing or teaching level. Leaders are instructed in the spiritual disciplines of prayer, fasting and Bible reading. They are taught core values, basic doctrine and techniques for understanding human personalities. They are given basic counseling skills, principles for productivity, warnings about potential dangers and principles for building personal integrity. Whether through weekly classes or seminars, leaders are transformed and informed about leadership qualities. They in turn are shown how to mentor another person in the personal disciplines of discipleship.

Level Four: Trained to Plant

The last level is the planting level, the highest form of leadership. Once people are trained to preach, pastor and prepare others, they are ready to begin planting a cell or releasing others to plant cells.

These four levels of leadership training can be recognized throughout the world by different titles, but the concepts remain the same: *evangelizing, assimilating, discipling* and *sending*. By concentrating your efforts on bringing each new believer down this track of leadership development, you will find a wealth of new leaders in your church within a matter of months.

Our leadership development efforts have paid off. From our 500 intercessors in the "Gideon's Army" prayer group in 1993, we now have more than 500 actual leaders! We meet monthly in a "Leadership Summit" in which I give them fresh vision, encouraging reports, goals to set and new leadership techniques to implement. Our goal is to have 2,000 leaders by the year 2000, each having completed our leadership track and leading a cell.

Every church can develop its own method of teaching the "four P's" as we refer to them: *preaching, pastoring, preparing* and *planting*. Bethany's leadership track lasts about nine months at which time a new believer is actually ready to open a cell. The methods, priorities and curriculum may vary, but the end result should be a sufficiently trained, gifts conscious, submitted to the vision, fruitful leader. Our training process includes large helpings of what I have come to refer to as the "Basic Eight."

THE BASIC EIGHT LEADERSHIP QUALITIES

After 20 years of pastoral ministry, I am convinced that leaders must develop and excel in the "Basic Eight" qualities in order to be successful.

1. Purpose

Leaders should be firmly convinced that their ministry and calling transcends any problems or other priorities. A sense of purpose is needed to guide leaders through the storms of life, provide them with a life mission and keep them on track. Much of Bethany's leadership teaching focuses on this area of vision because the seed of all motivation is found in *purpose.*

2. Priorities
The understanding of prayer and fasting is also essential to leadership. A ministry without prayer and fasting will quickly degenerate from *motivation* to *momentum* and will lack the energy and creativity to continue. John Wesley asked all of his pastors to fast two days a week. We find that believers in every part of the world who fast and pray will rise as leaders. The story of Mary and Martha (see Luke 10:38-42) and of the selection of deacons (see Acts 6) shows that our priority must be "ministering to the Lord and fasting" (see 13:2). Our leaders receive a suggested plan of prayer and suggested times for fasting weekly, monthly and annually.

3. Procedures
Moses built the tabernacle according to the "pattern shown you on the mountain" (Heb. 8:5), and God also has a pattern that He will show you concerning your leadership development and cell groups. It is important for every cell leader to follow the pattern the senior pastor and pastoral leadership have laid down. When that pattern is not followed, the cell ministry will "proliferate" into confusion. Cell reporting, meeting format and a host of other practical issues should be clearly spelled out and understood. Weekly records should be compiled into a report for the senior pastor to study so he has a quick understanding of problem areas each week.

4. Personalities
The four basic personality styles or temperaments have been studied for thousands of years. Practically every book on relationships and marriage today includes a study of these four personalities under different titles: lion, beaver, otter and golden

retriever, or choleric, sanguine, phlegmatic and melancholy.[4] They all describe the basic styles of a driving-oriented personality, a people-oriented personality, a security-oriented personality and an analytically-oriented personality. Because almost 70 percent of all people have a security-oriented personality and only 2 percent have a driving-oriented personality, it is important to know how the 70 percent will react in any given situation!

All of our cell leaders are trained to identify and understand the four basic personalities within their groups. Using this information, they are able to determine what each person's greatest fear may be in the cell. In fact, our cell members have all taken a personality inventory, and because they know themselves, are better able to relate to others' temperaments within their groups. Understanding the temperaments gives leaders the edge not only in cell-group dynamics but also in their families and at their places of employment.

5. Problem Solving

The nature of any endeavor is problem solving. Leaders must know how to attack a problem without denying its reality. They must possess the basic problem-solving skills of intuition, investigation, input, initiative and evaluation. In addition to solving personality problems, leaders must face logistical problems such as dealing with children, delegating to avoid leadership "burnout" and other such challenges. They must be aware of spiritual problems that may surface through greed, lust or pride.

Every cell leader should have training in the Scriptures and application to handle basic counseling situations that arise over finances, destructive habits, volatile emotions and domestic abuse. They do not provide "in-depth" counseling, but are a first line of treatment: "first aid" for the Body of Christ. Cell leaders don't give "pastoral counseling," but they do give "pastoral care." Of course, they understand that they have a great support structure in place if the problem is too overwhelming. Those who are supervising them know to refer individual, difficult cases to those with greater experience and gifting.

6. Producers

Cell leaders must be motivated to produce other leaders. Through the "Principle of Twelve" (see chapter 8), they are taught to isolate faithful men and women who can be their assistants. The primary spiritual goal of cell leaders becomes pouring their lives into those 12 people, coaching and mentoring them into fruitfulness. As we've already discovered, there is no better use of your time than to be developing others who will produce far more than you will in your lifetime.

7. Principles

Life should be built upon principles, not persons. The transcending values of commitment, honesty, family and purity are just a few of the ideals a leader must possess. These "core values" help the leader make decisions like a plumb line helps a builder to begin a straight wall. Leaders must be taught about their motives, integrity, finances and the priority of family over ministry. A solid foundation of principles will remain under the leader no matter how high that person rises in the kingdom of God.

8. Productivity

A psychologist at Stanford University tried to show that we live for productive results, or fruit. This researcher hired a man—a logger. He said, "I'll pay you double what you get paid in the logging camp, if you'll take the blunt end of this ax and just pound this log all day. You never have to cut one piece of wood. Just take the end that is blunt and hit it as hard as you can, just as you would if you were logging." The man worked for half a day and he quit. The psychologist asked, "Why did you quit?" The logger said, "Because every time I move an ax, I have to see the chips fly. If I don't see the chips fly, it's no fun."[5]

Bethany's productivity training for leaders involves the principles of setting long and short-range goals, personal motivation and encouraging skills, communication (and avoiding miscommunication), delegation (team management and "ownership"), and the principle of reward. By understanding these principles, leaders stand a better chance of being one step ahead of those they are leading, and reaching the goals of soul winning and leadership development.

"LEADERSHIP U"

Is your appetite whetted for training leaders yet? McDonald's has "Hamburger University," a school for would-be McDonald's managers located outside of Chicago. Anyone who is going to be managing one of its 2,100 stores around the world can graduate from "Hamburger U" and be fully equipped and confident. Why shouldn't the church have a "Leaders University" where everyone can enroll and develop their leadership skills?

Now that you know the basic values we use at Bethany for all leadership training, let's look at a simple way to present the concept of leadership to your church and to track its progress toward the goal of opening its own cell group!

Notes

1. Dr. David Yonggi Cho, *Successful Home Cell Groups* (South Plainfield, N.J.: Bridge Publishing, Inc., 1981).
2. Ibid. The Seven Dangers are identified by Dr. Cho as "Seven Obstacles" on pages 31-47. They are summarized here:
    1. The lack of training for the leaders.
    * The leaders did not know how to conduct a meeting or how to teach a lesson.
    2. The lack of discipline at meetings.
    * Hosts were attempting to outdo each other with meals and allowed meetings to go on too long.
    3. Unapproved outside speakers.
    * Without the pastor's knowledge, people were invited to speak, introducing teachings that were not in agreement with the doctrine of the church.
    4. Financial problems.
    * Cell members loaned one another money with interest. Others began promoting investment opportunities.
    5. Large, unmanageable groups.

* As they grew, some cell groups had 30 to 50 families.
6. Dishonesty in the collection of offerings.
* Occasionally, money collected for the church did not arrive at the church treasury in its entirety.
7. Division in leadership.
* Associates attempted to take away the cells they supervised to begin their own churches.
3. Dr. Sandy Kulkin, The Institute for Motivational Living, Inc., P.O. Box 925, New Castle, PA 16103; phone 1-800-779-3472.
4. The "lion, beaver, otter and golden retriever" analogies can be found in John Trent and Gary Smalley's book *The Two Sides of Love* (Colorado Springs: Focus on the Family, 1990). The "choleric, sanguine, phlegmatic and melancholy" analogies can be found in Tim LaHaye's book *The Spirit-Controlled Temperament* (New York: Walker & Co., 1986).
5. Illustration from John C. Maxwell, *Be All You Can Be!* (Wheaton: Victor Books, 1987), p. 21.

MULTIPLYING LEADERS

In chapter 6, we began the outline of a process based upon four purposes: *preaching, pastoring, preparing* and *planting.* In this chapter, we will further develop that outline.

We have discovered that most people think concretely rather than abstractly. Therefore, we find the model of a baseball diamond extremely helpful. I first saw this concept used in the materials of Dr. Rick Warren, pastor of Saddleback Valley Community Church in Foothill Ranch, California. We have modified the baseball diamond model to fit the cell model of the church. This model has become our method of teaching and leading people from the moment of conversion to their birthing as a cell leader (see diagram on next page).

Notice that these four purposes for leadership training are each assigned a "baseline." All four of the purposes end with an event, a tangible occurrence that signifies the conclusion of that phase of the person's growth in the cell process.

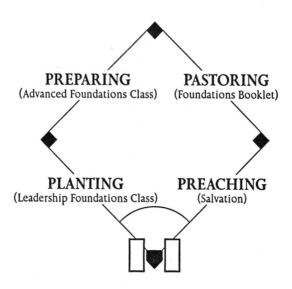

PREPARING
(Advanced Foundations Class)

PASTORING
(Foundations Booklet)

PLANTING
(Leadership Foundations Class)

PREACHING
(Salvation)

HITTING THE BALL

The process obviously begins with "preaching," a response to the gospel in some avenue of ministry. As soon as people respond to the *preaching* of the gospel in a service or a cell, our goal is to help them immediately understand that their new life in Christ will have stages of development.

When people respond to an altar call in a service, they are brought to a District Office where they view a short video from me, the senior pastor. I introduce the District pastor on the video as a close personal associate, because most of these people responded to a message from me and have no idea who or what a "District" pastor is. Then, I give them a short overview of cells by providing them with the "baseball diamond" brochure and explaining it on the video. People can clearly see that a "track" is being laid out before them and that they have simply hit the ball!

The counselor, who is a cell leader, has one objective at that moment: to *verify* each person's salvation experience. The counselor's objective is to give the new believer biblical assurance that Christ is now present in his or her life. Whatever personal problems the cell leader has ministered to are noted on the new believer's information card.

FIRST BASE: WATER BAPTISM AND CELL ATTENDANCE

Within 24 hours, a pastor and a cell leader make an attempt to visit the new believer. Their goal is to get the person to "first base," which is water baptism and cell attendance. Water baptism is the most important of the two at this point, because it helps to make the public profession of Christ firm. In addition, new believers are encouraged to attend a cell the first week they are converted.

The pastor and cell leader may have studied the problem areas that were listed on a new believer's information card, and may zero in on those problems to establish a communication link

> *Most of America's new converts do not endure because they never unload the "baggage of Egypt" before entering "Canaan."*

with that person. Sometimes, family members are saved during that visit. In Bogota, it is not uncommon for the "assimilating" visit to conclude with the opening of a new cell, right in the home of the brand new Christian!

SECOND BASE: PASTORING

After water baptism, the new believer heads toward "second base" by spending the next four to six weeks in a cell group learning the basics of Christianity from a *Cell Group Foundations Booklet.* Topics range from personal evangelism to the baptism in the Holy Spirit. The goal is to establish a pastoral relationship with the new believer. This second stage may be completed or even interrupted by the second great event in that person's spiritual development: a "First Step Encounter" retreat. Held the last weekend of every month, the retreat is the "B.C./A.D." of a new believer's Christian life.

Most of America's new converts do not endure because they never unload the "baggage of Egypt" before entering "Canaan." The retreat format is focused on a process called "soul therapy," a phrase coined by Dion Robert, the great pastor of the Eglise Protestante Baptiste Œuvres et Mission Church in Côte d'Ivoire, West Africa. The identical principle is used in Bogota where many who are converted have strong allegiances to demonic spirits, have endured family abuse and molestation, or have drug and alcohol bondage. Here in America, a dysfunctional generation has little concept of forgiveness and forsaking the past.

The "First Step Encounter" weekend begins on a Friday night and lasts through Saturday evening. We have found it works best if held at a retreat facility. The goals of the encounter include:

1. Helping new believers to relax and focus their minds on their spiritual lives;
2. Educating new believers about areas of bondage that may be in their souls, though the spirit has been forgiven;
3. Facilitating an intensive time of prayer, renouncing strongholds and praying for deliverance if needed; and
4. Ministering the truth to them about their position in Christ and the power of the Holy Spirit.

The retreat is administered by the pastors and selected cell leaders who have been praying and fasting over the people registered for the retreat. Initially, the retreat may be held at the church where food is easy to prepare and the participants return home in the evening to sleep. This arrangement has only limited success, however, since an important part of the *encounter* is to be away from phones, televisions and familiar home settings. The "First Step Encounter" weekend should be the conclusion of the assimilation or *pastoring* phase.

THIRD BASE: PREPARING

Because the "First Step Encounter" weekend takes place on the last weekend of the month, the following week begins the "Discipleship Class" at the church. Held on Wednesday evenings after the worship portion of our regular service, this 12-week class zeros in on major Bible doctrines, Bible study, prayer, spiritual warfare, identity in Christ, servanthood, the local church and finances. The new believer is now in the "preparing" stage, the part of the Christian life where he or she is taught the basic doctrines of the faith. Having successfully completed these 12 classes, the "preparing" stage ends with another event, the "Leadership Formation Retreat."

The "Leadership Formation Retreat" presupposes that a new believer has been through at least four months of pastoring and preparing. This person is now ready to be exposed to the fundamental aspects of leadership.

In a one-day-seminar setting, these *preparing* Christians are brought to the church District Office and taught by a District pastor about the many aspects of the cell church: the vision (*purpose, plans, goals, actions*); personal evangelism (*oikos*); the multiplication process; how to lead a meeting; components of a cell meeting; how homogeneous groups work; how to make a lesson applicable in different situations; three ways to multiply a group; techniques for raising up interns; and how to put cell members on the "baseball diamond" track toward leadership.

The importance of this one day "crash course" in cell leadership cannot be overstated. We have also made provision for "old-timer" disciples who have either transferred to our church or have just decided to become involved in leadership. The Bethany congregation understands that mature believers who are water baptized and grounded in the Word to the "third base" level can enter the leadership track at the point of a Leadership Formation Retreat. They go from the "dugout" to "third base"!

In this way, veteran church members who catch the vision of cells and multiplication can go straight from cell participation to cell leadership in a short period of time without taking months to cover ground they obviously already know. In fact, after this one-day seminar on cell leadership, they are adequately equipped to begin a homogeneous on-the-job cell or a family cell in a home.

The flexibility extended to veterans represents a "bias for action" in our structure. We prefer the "ready, fire, aim" approach because the new leaders will remain under the direct oversight of their cell leaders each week in their regular cell meetings. Only mature believers are free to open a cell group at this point, and if they do, they must continue to attend what we call the "Leadership Class."

HOME PLATE: PLANTING

The first four months of introduction now give way to serious training for all cell leaders, whether they are new converts or established disciples. This is the stage of "planting," three months of serious training that will set the stage for the rest of the leader's life. We have put together 12 classes, representing what we think are the most important areas in a leader's life (see the "Basic Eight" in the previous chapter). The 12 classes include:

- **Week one:** Covers basic counseling skills that we employ daily as pastors. This teaching would not include in-depth counseling, only "paramedic" level counseling for pastors to build upon if necessary.
- **Week two:** Teaching the principles of mentoring and building relationships such as those of Elijah and Elisha, Moses and Joshua, and Jesus and His disciples.
- **Week three:** Teaches the development of spiritual gifts in the leader and others, helping them to isolate their motivational gifts.
- **Week four:** Communication skills for effective listening and speaking are explored.
- **Week five:** Participants are trained in how to use per-

sonal evangelism skills, as well as how to help others share their faith in Christ.

- **Week six:** Personality types of the class members are discovered and discussed through the use of the D.I.S.C. personality profile test.
- **Week seven:** Teaches the ten leadership principles Jesus used in preparing His disciples for ministry.
- **Week eight:** Training in conflict management and confrontational skills.
- **Week nine:** Potential leaders are given principles for effective time management.
- **Week ten:** Practical ministry skills are identified for handling situations such as death, crisis and hospital visitation.
- **Week eleven:** Teaches "people" skills that help build relationships and encourage others.
- **Week twelve:** Gives practical advice on how to maintain a positive attitude in ministry.

These three months of training add years to a leader's spiritual maturity. Each class is taught by the very best leader on Bethany's staff in that particular area. The Leadership Class is also held on Wednesday night following the worship time of our regular service.

After seven months of assimilation, indoctrination and preparation, the new convert is ready to begin a cell. This "process" may seem long and arduous to someone reading about it, but the new believers' hunger and appetite for spiritual things brings them through it rapidly. In addition, they are part of a cell the entire time, continually learning in a "hands-on" way from the cell leader. The "process" of leadership development is absolutely essential both to properly ground new believers in the Word and to adequately train them for the time when they will begin to lead.

As a follow-up to the seven months of training, we have developed a monthly "Leadership Summit." The summit begins with breakfast on a Saturday morning, followed by an hour of intensive prayer for souls and harvest. The last hour includes a teaching from me, the pastor, during which I discuss the four topics for that month's lessons, explaining what type of person will respond best to an invitation to each lesson. Then, I cover some area of vision and leadership such as "David's mighty men," "Nehemiah's steps to leadership" and "avoiding miscommunication," to mention a few.

OUR FIELD OF DREAMS

Bethany's goal is to develop a Cell Leaders Institute where a leader could reenroll into enrichment classes for training in many different areas. The church-based Bible school idea is not new, but the nature of the cell structure surely demands it.

Dr. Cho has so refined his "in house" Bible College that many of his cell leaders have the equivalent of a seminary degree! The Charismatic International Church in Bogota also offers a three-year extended training school for its cell leaders.

Look at what this exciting leadership training process achieves: It takes a new believer and mentors that person all the way through Bible College where he or she is ready to go out and plant a cell in any city or culture of the world.

Once this process is in place, setting goals for multiplication in a year becomes very simple. If you want 50 cells one year from now, you must have at least that number of people at "second base" or beyond. Goals begin with *actions*, and until people are moving around the bases, certainly no one will reach home plate! Each overseer on staff should set a goal for the First Step Encounter retreat, the Advanced Foundations Class, the Leadership Formation retreat and taking the Leadership Class. Keeping track of each person's progress in this process is easy now that so much sophisticated computer software is available.

"Preach, pastor, prepare and plant" is a finely tuned process to conserve your hard work in preaching and equipping believers to do what you are doing. "Lift up your eyes" now as Abraham did and release your faith for children as many as the stars of the sky.

If you prepare the discipling process, God will be faithful to send you the harvest. Though some will drop out and never complete the process, at least you will have provided them with the opportunity. Out of this process will come LEADERS, precious leaders from every race, generation, denomination and gender. Are you ready?

Now, let's take the principles of multiplication and wed them together to our track of leadership development into the most powerful form of cell church growth ever developed: the "Principle of Twelve."

"BATTER UP!"

THE "PRINCIPLE OF TWELVE"

Your efforts toward successful leadership development will probably culminate in the same way Jesus' did: developing "twelve" selected assistants with whom you spend the majority of your time in order to help you carry out the vision. The "Principle of Twelve" is confirmed again and again throughout the Bible: The 12 patriarchs, 12 tribes of Israel, 12 apostles, 12 foundations in the heavenly Jerusalem and many other biblical references underscore the importance of this number as the number of "government."

Churches all around the world are finding that with groups of "twelve," the Great Commission can be easily accomplished. For example, Maiwa'azi Dan Daura from Jos, Nigeria, was one of the original leaders of Campus Crusade in Nigeria. His ministry began with 7 men whom he discipled. The goal of those 7 men was to find 12 others to disciple. Throughout the past 20 years, their little group has become a vast leadership "network" of "twelves" that has given birth to more than 1,200 churches in Nigeria. Every week, the students meet with their mentors and those they are mentoring.

Cesar and Claudia Castellanos began their small ministry, Mision Carismatica Internacional, in Bogota, Colombia, in 1983. After several years, their youth pastor, Cesar Fajardo, began a process similar to Maiwa'azi Dan Daura by discipling 12 teenagers in his youth group. Those 12 teens were in turn given the task of finding 12 other youth (ages 16-25) to disciple and release into ministry as their assistants. The huge pyramidal structure of ministry relationships has now reached three "generations" of "twelve," with some working on their fourth.

There are now 6,600 cell groups in the youth department at Mision Carismatica Internacional with the goal of having 10,000 youth cells! Every Saturday more than 600 new young people are converted in the Saturday morning youth service. It is not uncommon to see a young person 25 years of age overseeing as

The "Principle of Twelve" has changed the traditional concept of cell multiplication by offering the possibility of continued relationship AFTER multiplication.

many as 800 cells, using the "Principle of Twelve." The church now has 14,000 cell groups (growing from 4,000 cells at the beginning of 1995) and all of the leaders are arranged under each other in the "Principle of Twelve."

As we have seen from Jos, Nigeria, the "Principle of Twelve" will work when simply used as a leadership training structure. However, when it is wedded to the cell structure as it is in Bogota, the result is a natural union. Cells need leaders, and leaders need outlets for ministry. In Jos, Nigeria, that outlet has come by planting churches. In Bogota, the outlet comes through planting cells, and that understanding has lifted Bethany into a "second stage" of the cell multiplication.

PRESERVING RELATIONSHIPS THROUGH THE "PRINCIPLE OF TWELVE"

In chapter 5, we saw the traditional principles of multiplication: cells must *learn*, *love*, *link*, *launch* and *leave*. They may multiply numerous times, each time severing the relationships they have built. Soon, however, cell members tend to lose the motivation for multiplication because no one likes to succeed just to be able to start over again!

The "Principle of Twelve" has changed the traditional concept of cell multiplication by offering the possibility of continued relationship AFTER multiplication. The cell leader spawns, not just "two cells," but an entire network of cells under his or her leadership. The ability to retain relationships while multiplying powerfully affects the motivation level, and there is no limit to the productivity and influence of a person starting at the "cell leader" level.

FUNDAMENTALS OF THE "PRINCIPLE OF TWELVE"

This "Principle of Twelve" is dynamic and explosive yet simple to understand and implement. We can follow it easily if we understand the following seven basic principles:

1. Everyone is a potential leader.
This one statement defies the conventional wisdom about leadership and who may possibly have potential. A quick look around the room at a cell meeting can tend to discourage this idea: Some are shy, some are sloppy, some are struggling. However, we must remember that the crew God sent to David at the cave of Adullum was "in distress or in debt or discontented" (1 Sam. 22:2). This most basic principle of the "Principle of Twelve" is based upon

something we rarely see in American churches: radical repentance and severance from the bondage of the past.

American churches are filled with members who can barely "backslide" because they have never "frontslid." Their inward struggles, secret bondages, past rejections and dysfunctional family heritages keep them from ever even considering themselves "leaders." In the fabulous cell church in Abijon, Côte d'Ivoire, Dion Robert pastors 120,000 members in 8,000 cell groups. New converts go through what they call "soul therapy": a personal ministry time of renouncing past bondages, habits and hurts.

In Bogota, Colombia, each new International Charismatic Mission convert is brought on a retreat to deal with issues that would keep that person from becoming an effective leader. The two-day retreat is so life altering that it concludes with a session in which each attendee is given a package of encouraging cards, letters and cassette tapes from their friends and family back home. Needless to say, the person goes home CHANGED.

Knowing that everyone is a potential leader changes everything. Your goal as a cell leader is to challenge and believe in those God has sent you so they will take their rightful place as cell leaders. By loving them, listening to them and encouraging them, you are to so passionately instill the vision and confidence of God in them that they are ready to go "bear hunting with a switch!" One by one, barrier by barrier, they cross over into "leadership land" where they are winning souls and discipling others.

2. Everyone can disciple "twelve" people.

The first premise leads to the second: If everyone has the potential to be a leader, then certainly all are worth the major effort it will take to develop them. Jesus had the Twelve (ultimately 11 after Judas' betrayal) with whom he invested most of His time for three and a half years. He obviously chose 12 because it is the perfect number to disciple. Paul understood discipling, therefore, he had an apostolic "core" (such as Timothy) that traveled with him everywhere. They were constantly learning and observing his "doctrine, manner of life, purpose, faith, longsuffering, charity, patience" (2 Tim. 3:10, *KJV*).

The lifetime goal of developing "your twelve" becomes a tremendous challenge for leadership development. Through the process of time, circumstances and face-to-face mentoring, a person who may have been "going nowhere" suddenly becomes a person of purpose, ability and integrity. Your hard work and effort at developing these people begins to pay off as they seek for and begin to disciple "their twelve."

Imagine the fulfillment it must be in Bogota for the youth pastor of International Charismatic Mission to have started with only 60 youth and now see three generations of "twelves" functioning as the oversight for that mighty youth ministry.

3. Everyone is ministered to and then ministers.

"In and out" is a principle of life. Healthy plants draw in nourishment and then give out fruit. This is also a central premise of the "Principle of Twelve." For instance, the senior pastor provides a cell lesson and leadership principle which he teaches to his "twelve." They take the information they receive and then give it out as they teach their "twelve" that same week. "Teach what you are taught" goes from one group of "twelve" to the next throughout the course of a week.

Whether written or verbal, principles are passed down "generation to generation" to the lowest "generation" where actual evangelistic cells are taking place.

Everything above that lowest level is strictly leadership supervision, a process that lasts for a lifetime. Incidentally, after the evangelistic cells meet at the bottom "level," they receive an offering which is then passed "upwards" the following week as the "twelve" meetings take place! The lessons flow down from the church through the "twelve" meetings and the offerings rise up through the "twelve" meetings. (Bethany has never received offerings through its cells, but many churches worldwide do so very successfully.)

"Teach what you are taught" involves a powerful dynamic

which Paul described to Timothy: "And the things you have heard me say in the presence of many witnesses entrust to reliable men who will also be qualified to teach others" (2 Tim. 2:2). In this way, teaching does not stagnate in a notebook somewhere, but is immediately imparted to those looking to you for leadership. "Teach what you are taught" leadership training can go on in any culture of the world without telephones, zip codes or computers. It is the "face-to-face" and "heart-to-heart" method.

4. A person is in your "twelve" only when that individual has opened a cell group.
A person may be in your cell (simply a cell member) without being in "your twelve." The goal of discipling and leadership development is for that potential leader (cell member) to open his or her own group. This occurs after you have brought that person through retreats, basic discipleship and some kind of "Leadership School." This 9 to 12-month process prepares the individual to be effective (as outlined in the previous chapter). The cell member begins to lead a cell meeting when you feel that person is ready.

After opening a new group, the leader continues to return to his or her original "sending" cell, as it meets each week, for mentoring, encouragement and training. This new cell leader, or "Timothy," has everything now needed for growth: training (Leadership Class), opportunity (a new cell), and support (a "mother cell" from which that person has been sent). Often, the original cell leader will meet with those cell members who have opened groups for a half hour prior to the "regular" cell meeting to answer questions and give them more training. The goal is reached when EACH of that person's cell members has started his or her own cell. At that point the "sending" cell becomes strictly a leadership meeting!

5. Everyone should win souls and develop potential leaders.
Every pastor, leader and Christian should win souls—we have been commissioned to do so! Using the "Principle of Twelve," a

realistic goal would be to prayerfully bring at least "twelve" people to the Lord each year through personal soul winning. New converts join your cell and become potential leaders; potential leaders who open their cells become permanent leaders in "your twelve." Obviously, before long you will have filled all the leadership positions in "your twelve." Your cell meeting then becomes a "leadership meeting" where all of your leaders gather with you for encouragement and training.

Every new convert you win and disciple can then be "fed" into the cell of one of "your permanent twelve" who has opened a group. By helping them grow, you also grow, because once all of the positions in "your permanent twelve" are filled, the only way for anyone else to enter that group is for someone to leave, die or fall away. In that case, someone from a "twelve" under you would be raised up to fill that position. This process makes the group something that can be built upon for a lifetime if necessary.

With everyone pastoring "their twelve," there is no limit to productivity. People with initiative and spiritual gifts can develop as rapidly as desired without waiting for their mentors.

6. Cells open most rapidly when they open homogeneously.
The word "homogeneous" is defined by *Webster's Dictionary* as "of the same or similar kind or nature." Studies by noted church growth observer George Barna have shown that most Americans today find their relationships in their workplace, not in their neighborhood as in times past. Therefore, many cells may be opened quickly in the workplace or with an affinity group. Practically everyone in the cell group has a homogeneous, "similar kind," grouping in their life where they could gather at least four people together weekly for a "group."

If people are given proper curriculum for a variety of homogeneous applications (women's, men's, business and professional, seeker groups, etc.), in addition to the possibility of the regular cell lesson, they have great confidence to begin. They know they can rely upon the support and backup of their regular cell group to stand with them and give them advice. This perspective brings rapid multiplication, and means that groups do not have to sit and wait for traditional multiplication processes in order to multiply (see chapter 5).

7. "Your twelve" are your assistants.

You are not only discipling "your twelve," but they become your "assistants." In Bogota, each member of "your twelve" takes the primary role of the follow-up of new converts one month out of the year. "Your twelve" become your immediate "staff" to accomplish your tasks. The result should be that the leader of the "twelve" is more free for prayer and the ministry of the Word as was in the case of the deacons in Acts 6. This principle can work powerfully in a smaller congregation where the pastor is called upon to preach, visit, do maintenance, intercede, lead worship, do weddings and funerals, and a host of other responsibilities. By starting a "twelve," the pastor's responsibilities could be divided among those who desire to learn and serve. The pastor's "twelve" can each in turn open a cell and recruit leaders and servants in their cells.

A key in finding "your twelve" is to focus on three. Jesus had an inner circle of Peter, James and John. Your first goal should be to disciple three, and then to challenge them to each find three. As we observe in Jesus' ministry, His disciples easily recruited and discipled those they already knew. When each of your "three" finds their "three," your group of "twelve" is complete! It's exciting to watch people start to focus in on the leadership potential of others so they can grow beyond just a casual relationship with them.

ADVANTAGES TO THE "PRINCIPLE OF TWELVE"

Let's review some of the advantages to the "Principle of Twelve":

- *Relationships never need to be broken.* One of the flaws of much cell ministry is the loss of contact after multiplication. In the "Principle of Twelve," each newly birthed cell maintains a continuous contact with the "mother cell" for life. Leaders remain under the tutorship of the individuals who trained them. Months spent in bonding and building trust grow into an abiding working relationship. The "disciple" is free to go as far as his or her gifts will allow in multiplication and cells, yet the person never feels "uprooted" from the "mother cell."

- **Staffing needs remain much lower.** A tightly interconnected team of leaders requires far less "middle management" from the church's full-time staff. Oversight tends to come from the internal support of the group rather than an external "scaffold" of support. The complex web of relationships that forms builds "muscles and sinews" into the church Body, attenuating the need for full-time pastors. The church will always need full-time pastors for care and direction, but the absolute demand to expand staff is not as pressing in the "Principle of Twelve" structure.

  Zone and District pastors also feel released to pursue more avenues of cell growth than just the geographical areas they oversee. They can develop many different kinds of homogeneous groups and areas. The task of the Zone and District pastors is also to *win "twelve," find "twelve"* potential leaders and *develop "twelve"* permanent leaders.

- **No one's potential is stifled.** It is very important that people with potential don't feel the "glass ceiling." In the "Principle of Twelve," each leader has the potential to become a "leader of twelve" (all cell members having become leaders). As those "twelve" also disciple "twelve" and birth their own "twelve groups," the original cell leader can become a "leader of 144," or whatever level his or her motivational skills can bring! No longer do we hear, "I can't do it until...." Leaders can watch their original foundations of cell ministry be built upon for life rather than simply recorded as a multiplication.

The revival at Ephesus shook the entire continent of Asia Minor, and it all started with "twelve men." As we've just discovered, using the "Principle of Twelve," we can evangelize not only America but also resistant cultures of people such as the Muslims of northern Nigeria who have been penetrated by Maiwa'azi Dan Daura. "And all the men were about twelve" (Acts 19:7, *KJV*).

Are you ready to boldly start to make your church a training base in order to send those trained leaders to the world? If so, let's enter the final phase of this book and look at ways to overcome challenges with a discussion about square one: "transition."

TRANSITION

As I write this chapter, I am on an airplane, flying at 37,000 feet. About an hour ago, we encountered some minor turbulence. I don't like turbulence at all, but I'm thankful the plane is still moving in the right direction. It bounces and jerks a little, but the forward motion and thrust is still powerfully propelling us toward our destination. Skillful pilots somehow know how to steer away from turbulence by changing elevations, vectoring around storms and using other navigational means to overcome aerodynamic challenges.

Likewise, church leaders must also be prepared for the numerous challenges of spiritual "turbulence" we will encounter in flying higher than we have ever flown before in our local churches! The bottom line remains: we are moving forward.

SHIFTING GEARS

All forward progress requires shifts, transitions and stages. For instance, the shifting of gears in an automobile always requires a "clutch." Without the clutch, the teeth in one gear are forced into another gear, and the result can be noisy, grinding and even damaging.

Shifts in the church can also present a threat. "Change" is the greatest fear among the personality styles of 71 percent of the American population. Most Americans like the same old slippers, the same old jobs, the same leaders, the same order at McDonald's, the same parking places, the same pews and seats at church, and the same sense of routine about most everything else in their lives. Therefore, pastors must carefully navigate down the settled highways of almost 71 percent of their congregations, learning how to shift and transition without causing damage.

As Bethany shifted gears into the "cell church" paradigm, there were several points at which we applied the "clutch." My hope is that I will be able to help you shift through those points, knowing full well that we have undoubtedly failed at times to realize that we were grinding on someone's past security.

THE "CREDIBILITY" CLUTCH

The first "clutch" we used at Bethany was that of "credibility." The month in which we introduced cells in 1993 was the same month in which we paid off our 110,000 square feet of buildings and 100 acres of property—10 years before the mortgage matured! In that same year the Lord enabled us to give 1.3 million dollars to missions. Therefore, our church had reached a point of confidence in the direction and focus of its ministry.

Dr. Rick Warren has very creatively illustrated the way shifts and transitions affect our American churches. He says the leader holds certain "debits" and "credits" with his church. A "debit" is a direction the leader has led the church that ended in failure. A "credit" is a direction the leader has led the church that resulted in an obvious success. The congregation keeps an "account"! If the pastor's "debits" outweigh the "credits," that leader may find some resistance when announcing the move to a cell-based structure.

Bethany was not "broken," so everyone knew that it did not need "fixing." However, as the senior pastor, I knew that something within our church structure had to shift in order to pastor, evangelize and train leaders better for America's coming revival.

THE "GOVERNMENTAL" CLUTCH

This need for change led to the second "clutch": "working within your governmental structure." Government in the church is critical to success in any transition. Bethany's particular government has evolved throughout the 34 years it has been structured as a church, and yet it has always maintained one key element: "simplicity."

Flexibility with Accountability

Any governmental structure that totally restricts the pastoral leadership from implementing vision for the church is not of God. Someone said that Moses would still have been on the shore of the Red Sea if he had appointed a committee to recommend whether or not to cross! God raises up a Moses to lead and gives that person the vision and blueprint for the church. However, that person must also be accountable in order to prevent a reckless pursuit of things that are opposed to the Word of God. The key phrase, then, is "flexibility with accountability."

Presbyters

Bethany is structured to provide both flexibility and accountability. We have three outside pastors who serve as "presbyters," men over 55 years of age with at least 30 years of pastoral experience. The senior pastor is made directly accountable to the presbyters, even to the point of removing the pastor from the pulpit if he defaults morally, ethically, financially or biblically.

Elders

Another component of Bethany's government is three "elders," men who fulfill the biblical qualifications of 1 Timothy 3:1-7 and are in one of the "fivefold ministry" offices found in Ephesians 4:11. These men are generally the three leaders on our staff who all have years of pastoral experience.

Deacons

The final component is three "deacons," men who serve in the capacity of helping to govern the practical aspects of the church. The deacons assist in property acquisition and decisions that affect the church as a "corporation." As senior pastor, I form the tenth member of this "board of directors." Local business decisions can be made legally with a decision of the three elders, three deacons and myself.

Any grievance against me personally must be brought to the three presbyters. Spiritual decisions and ministry direction is never subject to the opinion of the deacons, only to the elders. This arrangement gives us the accountability needed without the stifling hindrance that comes when men who are "deacons" are asked to give spiritual oversight to a church.

Whatever your church government, be sure it contains both elements of flexibility and accountability. If your church foundation is wrong, every effort to change structure and direction will be difficult. The result could be similar to that of my friend who had a new home built. When the mason poured the foundation, the man was drinking heavily. Thus, the concrete was poured 17 inches out of "square"! Once it was done, it was done! As a result, every piece of plywood, Sheetrock, framing, cabinets, walls and carpet had to be cut on an angle. Unless your foundation is correct, the gears of transition will grind with frustration and effort as you try to accomplish whatever the Lord is leading you to do.

THE "JOY" CLUTCH

A third "clutch" Bethany used to transition smoothly is simply described in the word "joy." A primary feature of a life-giving church is that the people laugh a lot! There is no sense of pressure, control or manipulation.

I can best illustrate the way joy works by sharing the experience a friend had while touring on a bus in Israel. As my friend gazed out the window, he saw a flock of sheep with a man presumed to be their shepherd walking behind them. My friend commented to the guide, "I thought the shepherd walked in front of the sheep."

The guide replied, "Oh, that is not the shepherd, that is the butcher. The shepherd leads, but the butcher drives." I have never forgotten that illustration. Often we pastors "drive" people into change! Instead of gently leading through example and excitement, we choose the path of coercion and manipulation. Because of this tendency, I have instructed all of our pastors to be certain they maintain *the joy of the Lord* in all they do. When people come into church after a long day or week, the last thing they need to see is a pastor with a face "as long as a Missouri mule eating saw briars!"

We have much to learn about joy from the church in El Salvador. On a recent trip there, I discovered that in their large leadership gatherings for cell leaders, they call out exciting "cheers" that verbalize their goals: "Can we take this city?" is answered by a massive, "YES!" "Can we evangelize the lost?" is also answered, "YES!" For several minutes everyone rejoices in the victory that their cell groups will experience that week.

When asked about this practice, a leader replied, "If the Ephesians could shout for two hours to Diana, a false goddess, how much more can we shout for a few minutes to praise the true and living God?" We are not trying to get people "worked up" into something empty and hollow, but our work for God must be filled with joy. "Spirit-filled" cell leaders are productive cell leaders, and times of exuberant praise and prayer together help us to maintain a sense of forward progress, even in difficulty.

The attitude of joy must also be communicated from the pulpit. The pastor should be excited about the vision and communicate it with a positive, not a defensive, posture. Instead of "harping" on people who are not involved in cells, the pastor should rejoice with those who are involved and give a positive witness to the effectiveness of their ministries.

> *The old expression, "You can lead a horse to water, but you can't make him drink" should be modified to include, "But you CAN salt his oats."*

The old expression, "You can lead a horse to water, but you can't make him drink" should be modified to include, "But you CAN salt his oats." One of the ways that Bethany "salts the oats" is by including hilarious skits in many of our services that depict a typical member trying to decide whether or not he or she should become involved in a cell. The members, even those not in cells, laugh at the obvious objections and realize how good cell life would be for them.

I have decided to maintain my joy in ministry and pursue that joy all the way to heaven. No method or system is worth losing our joy over. Paul even said, "We are helpers of your joy!" (2 Cor. 1:24, *KJV*).

THE "SUCCESS" CLUTCH

A fourth element of successful transition is to "build upon success." Most major corporations have pilot programs and test markets to establish a new product in a new market. The same kind of market research may be needed to establish a new cell ministry.

Bethany began its cell transition from a proven base (the Gideon's Army prayer ministry) and could predict a high level of success in its ability to multiply. However, I know of a church that became excited about the cell vision and "assigned" all of its members to cells. With no proven track record or experience, some of the groups ended in failure after only a few weeks. The experience left a bad taste in the mouth of some of its members. Nothing succeeds like success! Begin groups that have a high probability to succeed. Leaders who are strong in prayer, strong in nurturing ability and strong in vision will make great initial leaders. You may ask, "What if I don't have ANYONE like that?" Start with prayer leaders. Then look for "pray-ers" who are "nurturers."

THE "VISION" CLUTCH

"Vision" is the clutch that allows your credibility, flexibility, accountability, joy, success and love to smoothly transition your church from where you are now to where you want it to be. As you spend time with the people who have a strong desire to pastor, nurture and help others, those people will catch the vision and the church will shift gears automatically.

Often, a pastor will mistakenly try to transition into a cell church by making all the "elders" (or deacons) cell leaders. We found that this approach did not work because these leaders were no more gifted pastorally than many other members in the church. They were good at practical "helps" as deacons, but were not necessarily good "nurturers." Let your elders get involved as they will, wherever they desire, but don't force them to lead just because they have previously been a part of the church leadership.

The danger place would be for a person who is a "leader" in the church to become antagonistic and negative toward the vision. If the focus of your cells is to disciple and nurture new converts and new members, there is nothing to "fight!" The problem comes when you coerce a member to join a cell or try to manipulate a present leader into becoming a cell leader.

Everyone wants to join success. The best advertisement is a satisfied customer! To properly transition, start with a core of leaders in whom you have total spiritual confidence: those with a mature devotional walk with the Lord and an outgoing personality to reach out and nurture others. Groups with this kind of a leader can hardly find enough chairs to seat the people who want to attend.

THE "PATIENCE" CLUTCH

Another necessary clutch that is needed to transition is spelled out in one word: "patience." I read once about a type of bamboo in Asia that grows only a few feet in the first four years, then suddenly shoots up to 90 feet in the fifth and sixth years!

I announced to our church that we were in a five-year transition process. Our initial growth was rapid as church members got involved. Our growth slowed in the fourth year as we ran out of leaders and learned the "Principle of Twelve." Our growth again lunged forward in the fifth year as homogeneous groups began to form within our geographical Districts.

In the same way, you can expect the Lord to show you little components of your structure that will help your cells to grow. Cell groups require hard work, much like farming! The book of James puts it this way: "Behold, the husbandman waiteth for the precious fruit of the earth, and hath long patience for it, until he receive the early and latter rain" (5:7, KJV).

Many pastors, however, have "Spiritual A.D.D." ("Attention Deficit Disorder") and tend to jump from "answer to answer." They become diverted to 25 other avenues of ministry (i.e., traveling continually, birthing personal programs, and becoming involved in boards and other organizations), instead of remaining totally focused on the cells. As a result, the sheep grow restless and confused. This problem can be alleviated by employing a tactic often used in the secular business world.

Most major corporations send their executives on at least a three-day outing each year to scrub floors, make hamburgers or do whatever that company does on a grassroots level. This "meeting of the customer" forces the people in leadership to encounter the real problems of their workforce rather than generating "ivory tower" decisions.

I recommend that every pastor lead a cell for a season and discover how it feels to have to stop at the store to buy corn chips before a meeting! Each little experience you have will be a rich teaching material for others and will show your "troops" that the "generals" are involved. Gradually, you will begin to see the major building blocks of your long-term leadership surface. One day, many of those you have met on the ground floor will be on your staff, so train them well!

THE "VISIONARY LEADERSHIP" CLUTCH

The last clutch to engage for a successful transition to a cell church has to do with an element of the pastor's personality: "visionary leadership." I have also heard this clutch referred to as "quarterbacking." Call it what you will: it is the ability to communicate a vision to a team and to inspire the members of that team to work together toward a common goal with excitement and motivation. Sadly, this element is not evident in many pastors. They are excellent as nurturers, have a good devotional life, but cannot seem to motivate anyone in the church to radically commit to volunteering for ministry opportunities.

When the apostle Peter tried quarterbacking, he usually put his foot in his mouth so much that he had "athlete's mouth"! At least, however, he could marshal the troops together into "one accord" and lead the charge against the enemy!

We all have different leadership styles, but I recommend that pastors take the "D.I.S.C." profile[1] and discover their personal styles: "Driver," "Influencer," "Steady" or "Careful." Styles, or combinations thereof, will come through in the way pastors transition. "Drivers" (2 percent of the American population) will bulldoze their way through, challenging the status quo and taking no prisoners. "Influencers" (11 percent of the population) are "people persons," talking and motivating but often short on particulars. "Steady" leaders (71 percent of the population) love the "well worn paths" and are uncomfortable stepping out into anything that is not "tried and proven." "Careful" leaders (16 percent of the population) are analysts, the "nuts and bolts" bean counters who love to refine the methods down to a carefully crafted system and process. My experience has shown that the most effective pastors in America are those with a combination of the "D-I" profile, "drivers" who are also "people" persons. If you find that you are not a "D-I," but rather a "steady" or a "careful" pastor, you should pair up in your church with an individual who possesses the "D-I" qualities as a "cell coordinator." Without a person who possesses these giftings, very little will happen and be maintained.

As you shift your church into a cell-based structure, check your "credibility," your "government," your "joy," your "patience" and your "visionary leadership." With these five factors in place and a large dose of prayer and fasting, something mighty will happen.

Are you ready for transition? Push in the "clutch" and shift gears. What you may have anticipated as a grinding, difficult period will actually be easy, exciting and exhilarating. As you begin, however, understand again that it is a "process" you will have to implement throughout the next few years. This "process" will be your key to successfully holding the massive harvest coming to America in the near future. Get ready to reap!

Note
1. "D.I.S.C." Profile is part of The Personality System, and is available through The Institute for Motivational Living. Inc., P. O. Box 925, New Castle, PA 16103.

DANGERS AND CHALLENGES

I once read a story about a construction worker who worked the night shift. The man was working high on an isolated part of the building when suddenly his feet slipped. As he began to fall, his fingers gripped the ledge. For an hour the man hung on for dear life while yelling for help. Unfortunately, the noise of nearby construction prevented others from hearing his cries of distress and the darkness prevented others from seeing his dilemma. When he finally reached a point of despair, his numbed fingers suddenly turned loose. Much to his chagrin, instead of plunging to his imagined death, the construction worker only dropped three inches to a scaffold below, which had been there all along!

CELLS SHOULD CAUSE SATAN TO TREMBLE, NOT THE PASTOR!

I can think of no better illustration to describe the sense of fear and phobia I often encounter when discussing cells with pastors.

Many have heard incredible "nightmare" stories of error, financial catastrophe, mass insurrection and church splits. Others have given their "best" to cells only to have had them sputter and fail. The mention of a cell church conjures up visions of fractured families whose partners are running off to meetings night after night while their children are neglected and marriages destroyed. Though any of these scenarios is a possibility, the hysteria that accompanies them has been grossly exaggerated by the devil. Satan FEARS cells because, as the world's largest churches have demonstrated, cells contain the most powerful principle to convert and disciple nations.

The element of the unknown is always present in a new endeavor, but the concept of home ministry is as old as the New Testament and just as powerful. However, because no picture is complete until it is framed, I feel it is important to discuss the difficulties Bethany has encountered along its five-year journey of transitioning to a cell church. This advance warning about the dangers and challenges lying ahead will hopefully prevent you from feeling like the construction worker!

THE SEVEN DANGER ZONES IN AMERICAN CHURCHES

I have isolated seven areas in which we have struggled the most during these past five years. Although the seven areas of Bethany's challenges closely parallel those listed by Dr. Yonggi Cho in his book *Successful Home Groups*, the challenges in American churches will be unique to the American culture.

Danger Zone #1: Spiritual Pride
The first challenge Bethany has faced is *an elitist attitude among cell members and leaders.* Spiritual pride is an ever-present danger which Satan promotes to bring division. "Di-vision" is a word meaning "two visions," and within a transitioning local church those two visions will be evident in people who have received the vision and those who have not yet embraced it. As we've discov-

ered in preceding chapters, the pastor is the key to helping the sheep relax and move through the process within their own comfort levels rather than trying to "drive" them against their wills.

Invariably, however, some well-meaning believers in the church will tend to become overzealous in their approach to recruiting "old-time" members into cells or into leadership. The "us versus them" mentality then develops, and a perfectly mature, well-balanced Christian begins to feel like an outsider in his or her own local fellowship.

When this kind of recruiting begins, the bottom line of cells which is to multiply life in the Body is eclipsed with a drivenness to build a church structure. Therefore, we have repeatedly instructed our leaders to reach out and minister, which is the true nature of Christ, rather than to build an organization or structure. Cells are simply a tool used to love, encourage and heal people, not a system to drive them.

Let the pastor be the motivator and "vision caster," because the pastor knows the pace at which the entire flock will move. I have on occasion given exhortations to our church about being one another's "friends" and not "advisers." Pride concerning titles, positions and results is always a threat, but wise leaders will themselves stay "flat on the ground" as Moses and Aaron did in the wilderness.

Danger Zone #2: Financial Impropriety

A second area of struggle for us has been in the financial area. A cell structure closely resembles a network marketing "downline," but some people have failed to see the difference! When they see a cell and its connection to other cells, their minds visualize instant access to hundreds of people who can be contacted with very little personal effort. Throughout church history, ambitious people with hidden agendas have felt that "godliness is a means to gain," and the loosely knit structure of most churches makes it difficult to penetrate these financial predators.

At Bethany, however, we have laid down a hard-and-fast rule that absolutely no business dealings are to occur within cells, period. No member or leader is permitted to use a contact with any other person for financial reasons. All financial indiscretion is subject to church discipline. Our leaders are highly trained in spotting a person who is using his or her cell connections for financial purposes and the leaders are quick to alert their cell members of our policy. Within the past five years we have only had perhaps three incidents of this kind of threat surface and all three were quickly squelched by the cell leaders, section leaders and Zone pastors.

In addition to restricting "financial farming" in groups, we also discourage the cells from getting involved financially in extensive support for benevolence and outside projects that are not connected to the local church. Although cells are free to receive occasional love offerings for a needy member, the leaders are instructed to watch for a person who is "freeloading" off the good intentions of the cell members.

Bethany gives more than 2 million dollars a year to missions. We channel most of our local assistance through our "Loaves and Fishes" benevolence store in the form of groceries, furniture, clothing and other household items, but we do not give direct cash contributions. Each District, however, does have a benevolence fund that it uses to disburse monthly to needy members. Therefore, most of our financial remuneration is channeled through the District Offices.

Danger Zone #3: Negating the Children

A third area of difficulty is usually one of the first questions raised about cell groups: What about the children? Visions of preschoolers running wildly about the homes of your best members is enough to discourage any smart pastor! I can honestly say that although the area of ministering to children is problematic, it has not been impossible to overcome.

We have made the presence of children a "drawing card" for parents. In one "Back to School" cell meeting, each child was prayed over by cell members. We had 2,500 children in cells that weekend and those children brought their parents with them! It suddenly dawned on us that one of the best ways to grow our family groups was to make ministry to children a strong point rather than a weak point in our structure.

We then connected our Sunday morning Children's Church lesson to some easy discussion questions for children in the cell meetings. Each week, different adult cell members rotate turns in taking the children into the backyard or into another room to cover the children's cell lesson with them. Of course, the children are free to come into the main meeting during the "icebreaker" and worship, and then leave during the discussion time.

Another consideration in dealing with children is to be open to other options. For example, some cell members prefer to pool their money in order to hire a young person to care for the children and teach the lesson to them. Other cell members have developed options that fit their style and age group even better.

One caution about children remains in all aspects of church-related ministry today: the threat of abuse. Ninety nine percent of this danger can be removed if you instruct your leaders to NEVER allow a young boy to care for the children during a cell. Bethany has adopted this policy in its church nurseries as well and has had no problems. Children should never be unsupervised. "A word to the wise is sufficient."

Danger Zone #4: Unapproved Teaching

A fourth problem we have encountered is the ever-present danger of cells providing a forum for those who wish to prey on the flock for their personal ministry. We have adopted, from Dr. Cho's experience, a policy of allowing no one to minister in our cells without pastoral approval. One of the ways we preclude wrong teaching in the cells is to have NO TEACHING! All of our groups are discussion groups, facilitated by a leader, not a lecturer. Therefore, there is no forum for a person coming in to present his or her latest doctrinal position on eschatology or freedom of the will.

As pastor, I have designed the lesson to complement what I am teaching the entire flock on Sunday and they have plenty to "chew on" in the lesson and application. In charismatic circles, the "parking lot prophecy meetings" can be a challenge as well when a "prophetic" individual wants to "give a word" to all present. Though we do not despise this very legitimate gift, it is to be given primarily where leaders are present to "judge" (the gathering of the local church) and not in forums where a leader may not be in the fivefold pastoral calling.

We do not allow books, tapes or newsletters to be distributed or promoted in cells. Any intervention of a spiritual emphasis into a cell is immediately reported to our pastors and it is judged in our weekly pastors' meeting. We have had virtually no problems with error being introduced, and only a few individuals have wandered from cell to cell seeking out a forum to teach or prophesy. I have marveled at the effectiveness of the pastoral supervision in such cases and in a few instances I have directed the staff in how to handle the individuals.

Danger Zone #5: Overlooking Our Needs to Be Real

The fifth problem we discovered is not a problem "generated" by cells but "exposed" by them. When you begin a cell group structure, you may be surprised to find out how much hidden sin

> As the relational "cauldron" heats up in a cell, the "scum" rises to the top to be removed. It may not sound pretty, but it sure is healthy!

there is in your church! America's churches are filled with individuals who have deeply rooted problems with pornography, X-rated videos, cocaine addictions, molestation and fornication, even abortion. Week after week, these hurting people attend church services and nod at the back of the person's head in front of them. However, when they become involved in a small group setting, they tend to want to unburden their souls and seek relief from their weighted consciences.

During the first two years of our cell groups, horrified leaders reported exposure of gross sin in our ranks. We thought believers were falling into terrible sin, when in fact they were falling out of it! As the relational "cauldron" heats up in a cell, the "scum" rises to the top to be removed. It may not sound pretty, but it sure is healthy! The beautiful part of this ugly scene is that people become part of a caring and supportive environment which helps them to walk out of their problems rather than attending a counseling session where they only receive instruction.

Whole families and marriages have been healed in cell meetings of problems that did not surface during our Family Conferences and regular services. The presence of God is truly visiting America now and our churches will soon be packed with repenting, renewed believers, longing for support and relationship!

Danger Zone #6: Backsliding and Burnout

In addition to exposing sin, we have faced a sixth challenge: leaders who have backslidden or burned out. Bethany now focuses closely on leaders who have done either. Earlier, we believed the myth that once people became leaders (cell or otherwise) they would be so caught up in the flow of ministry that they would never backslide! Not so! Cell leaders go through seasons of difficulty on their jobs, with their kids and in their finances. They may be tempted on the job or in a cell relationship.

At first we were appalled when an actual cell leader fell into sin! Then, we realized that ministry does not exempt anyone from the possibility of sin, not even in greater doses. In fact, all leaders become the prime targets for Satan's temptation as illustrated in David's tragedy with Bathsheba. We have instructed our leaders in the ministerial ethics of never being alone with a member of the opposite sex, never visiting in a home without a partner and quickly assessing the appearance of any situation.

Just as cell leaders are not exempt from temptation, they are also not exempt from burnout. Leadership "burnout" has only occurred on a small scale in the past five years, but it almost always can be traced back to a weak devotional life. Someone pointed out that when you are "de-plenished," you must be "replenished."

Elijah's victory on Mount Carmel left him an open target for burnout under the juniper tree in the desert. We have taught our leaders that they have a responsibility to spend time each day sitting at the feet of Jesus. In both Bogota and Seoul, each cell leader spends a minimum of three hours a day in prayer. Unlike Bogota and Seoul, we do not mandate a time period, but we do challenge our leaders to be consistent in their devotional time. We know that "those who wait on the Lord shall renew [Hebrew: 'change'] their strength" (Isa. 40:31, NKJV).

We also teach the cell leaders to constantly assess their priorities. During the summer, for instance, baseball, T-ball, softball, cookouts and "chill-outs" are popular. We accommodate the desire to maximize summer by having several "outdoor" cells and barbecues. However, we remind our leaders to pace themselves and not to allow all the outside opportunities to eat up their time. Most Americans have more opportunities than time, so they must wisely discern what activities are most "important."

I have used the following illustration of a "Cross road" with our leaders. The world and even some Christians have chosen a road on which they can voraciously pursue the goals of ease, relaxation and retirement. Their idea of the "good life" is to be independent, financially solvent, able to travel anywhere and be retired golf addicts by age 45.

The other road is the road of the Cross. Christ spent His 33 years of life pursuing ministry and serving others. The "Cross road" is the road of giving, working for the Lord and redeeming your earthly time for ministry. Pleasure is not the goal, but true fulfillment is found when fruit comes to maturity in the Lord.

No one can be moving down both roads at once: Every individual must choose the road he or she will pursue. If this "core value" is not settled in your leaders, you will constantly find

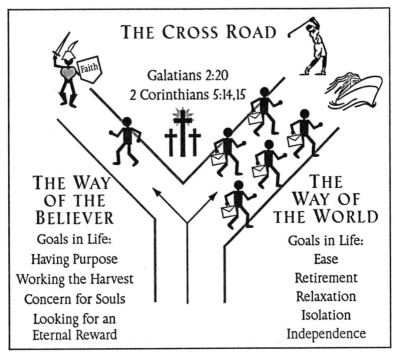

THE CROSS ROAD

Galatians 2:20
2 Corinthians 5:14,15

THE WAY
OF THE
BELIEVER

Goals in Life:

Having Purpose

Working the Harvest

Concern for Souls

Looking for an
Eternal Reward

THE
WAY OF
THE WORLD

Goals in Life:

Ease

Retirement

Relaxation

Isolation

Independence

them making choices that push the priority of their ministry further down the line. We have found that weekly "huddles" with section leaders or Zone pastors outside of their cell meetings keep cell leaders focused on their priorities and refired to win souls and maintain the vision.

Danger Zone #7: Proselytizing

A final danger we have encountered is the issue of "proselytizing." Overzealous members have approached members of sister churches in an effort to recruit them for cell attendance or even cell leadership. Needless to say, proselytizing does not go over favorably with other pastors and has a negative impact on others in the kingdom of God. Bethany has instituted strict policies in this regard. For example, no one is allowed to attend one of our cell meetings without the approval of his or her pastor, either in writing or by phone.

Some pastors who don't have cells have been open to encouraging their members to attend (but not many!). At Bethany we stress that we are not looking for "transfer growth," but for "conversion growth." A copy of our policies and training for cell leaders is mailed to any concerned pastor and that information generally stops dissension.

In spite of all our efforts to stop attendance at cells by members of other life-giving churches, some sheep have "jumped the fence" in pursuit of the cell vision. Someone said, "We don't steal sheep, but we do grow grass!" Just as I'm sure we have had some people depart who disagreed with our vision (though I cannot recall a single one), some have also come to Bethany to be a part of it.

Bethany's policy is to encourage the fence jumpers to return to their churches, but we cannot force them. We do, however, inform their pastors when they belong to sister churches. We also ask them to simply join a cell and remain there for some time before pursuing leadership. We call it "sitting and soaking" for a while as we observe their lives and gifts among us.

Perhaps as you have read this list of seven danger zones, you have felt your spiritual fingers "losing" their grip one at a time and felt as though you were falling! Remember, "underneath are the everlasting arms" (Deut. 33:27). This list of seven danger zones does not exhaust all of the issues we have dealt with or will deal with in the future. However, most of these issues involve just plain old pastoring people.

We have never faced mass insurrection, deception or exodus by caring for people through cells. In fact, we have exploded with growth by closing the "back door" through which they were pouring out from lack of pastoral oversight. Be prepared and vigilant for these possibilities but not paralyzed by fear. Listen to the voice of the Holy Spirit and proceed in the direction He leads you.

Having isolated our fears and prepared ourselves for dangers, let's prepare for the greatest harvest in the history of the world. Millions are about to be saved in America and God is preparing the cell church like an ark of safety for a godless generation's awakening to the turn of a millennium and signs of Christ's return. Get ready for massive growth! Our job is not to prepare for disaster but to prepare for His coming!

TO INFINITY
AND BEYOND!

The famous phrase "To infinity and beyond!" shouted by Buzz Lightyear in the movie *Toy Story*, has been immortalized as the battle cry of boundless optimism. As we conclude this book, some perspectives about the powerful reality and future possibilities of the cell church are in order.

First, a perspective on "people." Our talk about church structure and ministry should always end with "real life" individuals whose lives have been dramatically altered by cell-church life. At Bethany, we don't have to look much further than Marion Slaton's life for such a miracle.

MARION SLATON

Marion's job brought her from New Jersey to Baton Rouge, and she arrived in the city not knowing a soul. A coworker told Marion about our church and invited her to visit. She attended service one Sunday, and a few days later, Janice Hall, a lady from

Bethany, called to schedule a visit with Marion in her home. A date was set. Janice stopped by Marion's house with a gift (a *One Year Bible*) and prayed with her, inviting Marion to attend her cell group. Marion was hesitant to get involved. She had recently separated from her husband and was hurting—something she

> *"I never experienced anything like it before. There was a lot of light, and a lot of happy, joy-filled people."* ...That is cells!

preferred to do in private. Janice was persistent and even volunteered to drive Marion to the meeting. Feeling cornered, Marion agreed to go.

What was it like? Marion said, "I never experienced anything like it before. There was a lot of light, and a lot of happy, joy-filled people who were comfortable with one another. They loved me...hugged me...and prayed for me. I was broken and didn't think I could be healed."

A change began to take place in Marion's life. As she continued to attend that cell group, she became more and more involved in the lives of others. Soon, Marion was hosting the cell meeting at her house, and she believes the group left an "anointing" in her home.

"I've seen signs, wonders and miracles as a result of the cell group, and I, myself, have received the inner healing I needed through the cell-group ministry," says Marion. "It was hard to be a single parent in a city where I had no family. My cell group gave me a family. They loved me, took care of my daughter when I traveled and gave me the support I needed."

Marion has gone on to be trained and has served as a cell leader. That is cells!

SOMERSET, KENTUCKY

In addition to Marion, my mind goes back to the story of a cell church in Somerset, Kentucky. A member of a cell was diagnosed with cancer. When she checked into a local hospital for her first round of chemotherapy, her fellow cell members, distraught at the plight of their "partner," met to discuss ways to minister to their sister. Their solution? They decided to buy her a wig and then told her they would also wear wigs at the point when she would have to wear one. The ladies are all supporting her, staying in touch with her daily, and even now, are willing to wear a wig to help her.

They all sit right together in church, making sure her every need is met. That is cells!

CELLS IN INTENSIVE CARE

Finally, in the fall of 1997, the daughter of one of our cell leaders mysteriously slipped into a coma. As a nurse herself, she understood the seriousness of the situation as eight specialists attempted in vain to determine why her daughter's vital organs were shutting down and her body needed life-support systems. From the first of September through the middle of October, her daughter was suspended between life and death, actually dying so many times the doctors stopped counting.

Every four hours, members of the mother's cell group held a prayer meeting in the intensive care room. Day after day, week after week, nothing changed. Suddenly, one morning, the daughter woke up! A miracle had occurred, and throughout the next month the daughter gradually improved. Still with no diagnosis, the doctors merely removed the life-support systems as she gained strength. Finally, after three months, the daughter was released and has fully recovered!

The daughter stood on the platform of our church thanking our members for their prayer support, but most of all thanking her mother's cell members who came month after month, every four hours to pray for her life. That is cells!

AMERICAN CELLS ARE AFFECTING
CHURCHES WORLDWIDE

A second perspective we should consider regarding the future of cells is how this new movement among American churches is affecting the growth of churches worldwide.

In January of 1995, I sat in a restaurant in Orlando, Florida, with a young pastor from Johannesburg, South Africa. His church had several thousand members but had not experienced consistent growth for several years. His desperate cry was to minister better to his church, so our conversation drifted toward Bethany's cell structure.

Although this young pastor had already investigated several cell churches around the world, he was excited about the possibility of visiting Bethany. How surprised I was when he informed me that he would fly home that weekend to Johannesburg and return the following Tuesday to attend our next Cell Church Conference! His return with several associates demonstrated a hunger for implementing the cell-church concept. He returned with fresh vision to Johannesburg and in his own words:

I was very impressed with what I saw. The pieces of the jigsaw puzzle became very clear to me. What my team and I learned from your church, we put into practice with great success. That same month we launched 100 cell groups. Within six weeks our attendance was up to 1,000 people actually attending cells.

Here we are now at the beginning of 1998, with 425 cell groups and well over 7,000 of our members belonging to cell groups. We have an actual attendance each week of 4,300 in cell-group meetings. Our goal for this year is to be very close to 600 cell groups with well over 6,000 attending those meetings in any particular week. I would like to take this opportunity to personally thank you for your contribution towards the success that we are enjoying.

The cell-church movement is sweeping South Africa as hundreds of churches have transitioned to a cell structure. Many of the new congregations in Russia have also been birthed as cell churches. Our church administrator flew to Novosibirsk, Siberia, for a cell conference to train a church which at that time had 4 cell groups. One year later, that pastor visited Bethany and his church has since grown to 80 cell groups! From Moscow to Siberia, the mighty Russian church plants are growing as a result of the "cell church" vision.

Our annual Cell Church Conferences are consistently attended by pastors representing as many as 15 nations. From Switzerland, Panama, Hungary, Cameroon, Malawi, Mongolia, India, Nicaragua, Russia and Zimbabwe, they come to understand how to pastor their people more effectively. Consistently, we hear reports of how these concepts have dramatically changed their churches.

One of our missionaries, David Pursiful, pastors a church outside of Guadalajara, Mexico. His church of 60 members grew from 4 cells in 1994 to 200 cells by 1997! Mexican churches in Mexico City, Monterrey, and throughout Mexico report tremendous growth in cells with one organization counting a thousand cells in their groups of churches alone.

Another one of our missionaries, Donald Matheny in Nairobi, Kenya, has reported phenomenal cell-church growth as well. He visited Bethany with a team of his Kenyan staff pastors from the Nairobi Lighthouse Church in November 1993. They returned to Kenya and began their cell ministry with 94 groups in August 1994. Their growth has been phenomenal!

They have been forced to move to the Nairobi City Stadium where each Sunday more than 3,500 people fill the stadium for three hours in their "cell-ebration!" They now have more than 500 cells and are only going to "allow" 250 of them to multiply in 1998, so the quality of their leaders remains high! This church is now impacting all of East Africa as pastors from Uganda and other East African nations are observing the revival at Nairobi Lighthouse and are transitioning to a cell-church structure.

THE PROPHETIC VISION

The last perspective I would like to give toward "infinity and beyond" is the prophetic vision that we at Bethany have for multiplying cell churches in America.

I will never forget my recent trip to preach at a Missions Conference in Nashville, Tennessee. As Melanie and I were praying quietly on the side of the auditorium during an altar ministry time, a person strongly used in prophetic ministry (and recognized as such by that local pastor) stepped up beside us. He asked if he could pray for us, and as he did, he began to give us a message from the Holy Spirit. Not knowing him, I was courteous and permitted him to pray, but only began to be interested in his "message" when he started speaking about things he could never have known anything about at all!

He said he saw us with an "eye dropper" in our hands. We were going to be used, he said, by the Lord to restore a "clear vision" to the church. In fact, he said it was a "20/20" vision, an "Acts 20:20" vision. He seemed unaware that Acts 20:20 refers to the meeting of the church in the home: "I kept back nothing that was profitable unto you, but have shewed you, and have taught you publickly and from house to house..." (KJV). He continued his word to us with a description of the "other boats" that came alongside the boat Christ was in (see Mark 4:36). He said the Lord had revealed to him that we had received an "anointing for multiplication" from a church in South America (we understood that to be the church in Bogota, Colombia), and that we would be used in the Western Hemisphere to help "other boats" receive that same anointing.

Numerous other details accompanied this word from the Lord, details that minutely described other relationships we had and the current and future status of our Bethany Cell Church Network. This network perfectly fit the description of the "other boats" that God would be sending alongside our church to be encouraged in their own cell ministries.

In January 1998, B.C.C.N. was formed to bring our national

cell-church conferences to 24 regional locations per year. In addition, a local resident staff was put in place to field questions, give advice and encouragement to the hundreds of new cell churches springing up all across America. Finally, materials and resources generated monthly in our cell-church environment would be made available to each B.C.C.N. church to keep them abreast of "cutting edge" materials both from Bethany and other cell-church ministries. The monthly "Leadership Summit," the four cell lessons per month, booklets that take believers around the "baseball diamond" toward leadership, and many other resources are provided to the "other boats" who affiliate with Bethany Cell Church Network.

Having no American model to follow, Bethany is a pioneer in the cell-church ministry, preparing a path for others to follow. Yet, as pioneers, we often have to assess the trail we are blazing, asking God for wisdom and guidance. Our cell structure and training methods are continually being evaluated and adjusted as the Holy Spirit directs.

Our hearts' desire as we enter the twenty-first century is to be a simple tool in the hand of the Lord to help the churches of the Western Hemisphere find the life-giving principles of cell-church pastoring that other churches worldwide are enjoying. What will the next millennium hold? Where will our nation be in 5 to 10 years?

In my heart of hearts, I believe we will be in "harvest" and "hostility" as a post-Christian society gropes for reality and casts off our biblical moorings. When these things happen, the "root structure" of thousands of Western Hemisphere cell churches will be deep and relational instead of shallow and sensational.

These churches will be built upon the principle of "family" and not just "knowledge" or "ministry." The Greek model for maturity was based on knowledge, but the Hebrew model was based on relationship. Cells build "family" into a church, making the members "sons and daughters" in the house, and not just "servants" in the house. They develop ownership, initiative, connection and security. Like Ezekiel's mighty army, their connection together will bring the breath of God and a greater "life" for the unsaved world to see.

THE FINAL FOCUS

The final focus of the cell church, I believe, will be the unreached people groups of the world. Bethany's Missions Department, in conjunction with the A.D. 2000 Movement, has recently completed a four-page "profile" on each of the 1,739 least evangelized people groups in the world.

Cell churches worldwide are adopting these people groups, assigning 10 cell groups to pray for each unreached people group. Through the use of a "prayer profile," the cell members see a picture of a person from that people group, relevant cultural and historical data, the latest status of missions work among them and prayer points for specific spiritual targeting. The goal is that the churches whose cells are adopting these people groups will then send a team of their best leaders to penetrate that people group and plant a cell congregation among the group by the beginning of the year 2001.

It's happening, now. The end of the Great Commission is upon us, perhaps even in our generation. The fruit of the final great world revival will be preserved in churches that have learned the secret of holding the harvest in small relational groups like the one that became entwined around the Messiah 2,000 years ago. Get your church ready for this final outpouring...find your prayer nucleus, train your leaders, focus on the new converts and prepare for multiplication. America is ready for revival...will WE be ready for revival?

APPENDIX

An Ideal Cell Meeting

What exactly takes place in a cell meeting? As I mentioned in an earlier chapter the formats of an edification and evangelistic meeting differ slightly because of the presence of unbelievers at an evangelistic meeting. However, I think a skeleton outline of the components would be helpful.

We have discovered that it is best to always start with FOOD! The first 20 to 30 minutes should begin with two people bringing a light snack (cookies, chips, etc.) and "snacking" around. We prefer not to have heavier foods and meals because it puts pressure on everyone to "perform" socially every week. However, there is something about starting a meeting with eating that relaxes everyone and gets them "in the mood." Groups that meet on the job or during lunch breaks eat together every meeting anyway, and of course adjustments have to be made in a setting where eating is impossible.

Sometimes, in a home setting, everyone will move into the living area and begin the "icebreaker" as naturally as any other topic of conversation. The group leader poses a simple question (written into each lesson) to which anyone can have a quick or humorous response. An "icebreaker" is indispensable because it promotes group community as well as opens up the members to sharing. During an "edification" type meeting (no unbelievers present), the group will spend 10 to 15 minutes at this point with worship. In fact, we have designed short worship tapes that lead a group through about four worship choruses for this very purpose. Otherwise, a member may lead with a guitar, keyboard or "acapulco!"

The next component is a discussion of four questions based around a passage of Scripture. Our groups generally discuss the topic from the previous Sunday's sermon. Both the sermon and the lesson parallel the readings in the *One Year Bible*. (Regal also published our daily devotional guide to the *One Year Bible* entitled *The One Year Devotional*.) Our goal is to have a cross fire of discussion, not a pyramid of teaching from teacher to student. Therefore, the "facilitator" (group leader) merely introduces a question and lets the group give their input. The lesson closes with an "application" in which the members group together into prayer triplets and pray about a practical aspect that the lesson has brought to bear on their lives.

After the lesson, the group focuses again on prayer and "vision." A white board displays the names of the people targeted for salvation by each group member. They spend time praying for the names on the board and discussing who they will invite to the next week's "evangelism" meeting. This format would obviously be used only when the unsaved are not present. We prefer to have the meetings last no longer than 90 minutes, believing that the predictability of the time frame assures greater participation. Some workplace groups meet in as little as 30 minutes, but one hour seems to be standard for a meeting before, during or after work. Each meeting, wherever and for however long it lasts, should answer positively to these four questions: Was there fellowship? Was there discussion? Was there application? and Was there vision?

How to Pray
for Unreached
People Groups

We know how many unreached people groups there are. In addition we know where they are and specific ways that we need to pray to bring them into God's family.

The **Unreached Peoples Prayer Profiles** are research reports that spotlight the remaining, least evangelized peoples of the world. Each report includes four pages of quality information, a regional map, up-to-date political and cultural data and a concise, well-researched, cultural description that explains who the people are, how they live, and how to pray for them.

Full sets of **Unreached Peoples Prayer Profiles** (covering all 1,739 Unreached People Groups) are available through Christian Information Network (CIN) for $99 plus shipping. CIN can be contacted at 1-888-772-9104 or by e-mail at 1kayes@cin1040.net.

For orders of 100 or more copies of individual profiles (not the complete set) call: 1-888-300-7800.

For more information:
Call: 1-504-774-1700 **Visit:** www.bethany-wpc.org
Write: BCCN • 13855 Plank Road • Baker, LA 70714

Join us in evangelizing the world!

Network with 2,000 Cell Churches Around the World

Pastor Larry Stockstill Invites You to Join the Bethany Cell Church Network

Here's what members of the Bethany Cell Church Network (BCCN) receive:

Church Memberships

- An audio-cassette of Pastor Larry Stockstill's monthly *Leadership Summit* message

- A copy of each of the four weekly cell lessons for the month

- A copy of each of the four sermon outlines that relate to the weekly cell lessons

- Monthly insights and world report on cell church-related issues

- A toll-free hotline to speak with BCCN staff pastors for answers to pertinent questions about cell groups

Individual Memberships

- Four monthly lessons
- Four monthly insights and world report
- An audio-cassette on a cell group leadership topic

Stay in tune and in touch—become a BCCN member.

For more information:
Call: 1-504-774-1700 **Visit:** www.bethany-wpc.org
Write: BCCN • 13855 Plank Road • Baker, LA 70714

JOIN NOW!
To receive your free cassette: "The Cell Church in America" By Larry Stockstill

NOTES

NOTES

NOTES

NOTES